How to
Buy Jewelry
Wholesale

HOW TO
BUY JEWELRY
WHOLESALE

FRANK J. ADLER

First Edition

HOUSE OF COLLECTIBLES
THE BALLANTINE PUBLISHING GROUP
NEW YORK

Important Notice. All of the information, including valuations, in this book has been compiled from the most reliable sources, and every effort has been made to eliminate errors and questionable data. Nevertheless, the possibility of error, in a work of such immense scope, always exists. The publisher will not be held responsible for losses that may occur in the purchase, sale, or other transaction of items because of information contained herein. Readers who feel they have discovered errors are invited to *write* and inform us, so they may be corrected in subsequent editions. Those seeking further information on the topics covered in this book are advised to refer to the complete line of *Official Price Guides* published by the House of Collectibles.

Copyright © 1998 by Frank J. Adler

All rights reserved under International and Pan-American Copyright Conventions.

H
C This is a registered trademark of Random House, Inc.

Published by: House of Collectibles
The Ballantine Publishing Group
201 East 50th Street
New York, NY 10022

Distributed by The Ballantine Publishing Group, a division of Random House, Inc., New York, and simultaneously in Canada by Random House of Canada Limited, Toronto.

http://www.randomhouse.com

Manufactured in the United States of America

Library of Congress Catalog Card Number: 98-96027

ISBN: 0-676-60126-X

Text design by Holly Johnson
Cover design by Kristine V. Mills-Noble
Cover photo by George Kerrigan

First Edition: September 1998
10 9 8 7 6 5 4 3 2 1

In memory of my parents, Erna and Felix Adler, who would have enjoyed reading this book. To my friend Cliff Gardner, who encouraged me to write, and to Goldie, whose company I miss.

Contents

Acknowledgments

This book would never have been completed without the participation and cooperation of the following people:

My editor, Randy Ladenheim-Gil, whose vision and courage allowed her to purchase this book and skillfully bring it to a successful conclusion.

My agent, Jane Dystel, who liked the concept the first time we discussed it, encouraged me to pursue it, and successfully brought it to the market.

To my wife, Bella, whose advice, constant help, and encouragement allowed me to finish this book.

Vicki Morrison, Kim P. Cino, Judy Colbert, Bruce Lanzl, and Jenifer Butters of *The Gemological Institute of America*, who gave so generously of their time, knowledge, and experience. Additional thanks to *The Gemological Institute of America* for contributing all of the photographs used in this book.

Martin Rapaport and Eli Borochoff of *The Rapaport Diamond Report* for allowing me to reprint their wholesale diamond price list.

Special thanks to Kathleen Olsen, who consistently offered encouragement, advice, and corrected my horrible grammar.

Peter Yantzer, *American Gem Society Laboratories*;
Dr. R. R. Harding, *Gemological Association of Great Britain*;
James V. Jolliff, *National Association of Jewelry Appraisers*;
Shoichi Toyoda, *Gemological Association of All Japan*;
Kenneth Scarratt, *Asian Institute of Gemological Sciences*;
Lloyd Jaffe, *American Diamond Industry Association, Inc.*;
Christian A. Coleman, *International Society of Appraisers*;

Richard Youmans, *American Jewelry Manufacturer*;
Linda Meehan, *Silver Trust Institute*;
Ami Johnson, *Modern Jeweler Magazine*;
David S. Atlas, President of *D. Atlas & Co.*;
Joseph W. Tenhagen, G.G., F.G.A.;
Richard B. Drucker, G.G.;
Dr. Melvin Poveromo, D.D.S.;
Clara Weinerth, Graphic Artist.

HOW TO
BUY JEWELRY
WHOLESALE

Somebody Has to Pay for All of This, but It Does Not Have to Be You!

Would you like to know what your most expensive piece of jewelry is really worth? Never mind what you paid for it or what your insurance appraisal says it's worth but the amount of cold, hard cash you could get if you needed to sell it today. The easiest way to find out is to offer to sell it to a retail jewelry store or pawnshop. I think you'll be angry and disappointed by the amount you are offered. You'll think you were ripped off when you bought the item, and you probably were.

One of the most appalling cases I personally witnessed during my twenty-five-year career in the jewelry business occurred in Fort Lauderdale, Florida. The store, located in a heavily trafficked, fashionable shopping mall, was large, well-staffed, tastefully decorated, and had an extensive inventory of fine jewelry and watches.

A man in his twenties wanted to sell a diamond engagement ring that he had recently purchased from the store. Apparently the relationship had ended and he no longer wanted the ring.

The store owner read the original sales receipt and examined the diamond with a ten-power magnification instrument called a loupe. After he was satisfied that the merchandise was authentic and it had been purchased from his store, he offered $450 for the ring.

The young man was shocked by the amount. He had paid $3,000 for the ring six months before! How could it only be worth $450?

Reacting to the customer's obvious displeasure, the owner

explained the economic facts of life. The cost of operating the store was enormous. The rent, salaries, benefits, advertising, utilities, professional fees, license fees, and city, county, state, and federal taxes accounted for 65 percent of the retail price of the ring. In dollar terms that meant that $1,950 went towards the expense of operating the store.

The diamond engagement ring was purchased by the store from a local manufacturer for $750. Adding up the cost of overhead, which was $1,950, and the cost of the ring, which was $750, the total was $2,700. The store's net profit on the sale was $300, or approximately 10 percent.

The customer still didn't understand the offer. If it cost the store $750 to purchase the ring from a manufacturer, why was the offer only $450? Shouldn't the offer have been closer to the cost of the merchandise?

The owner explained that when he bought diamonds from a merchant, or a ring from a manufacturer, he had anywhere from 60 to 180 days to pay for it. Even after the grace period had ended, he could sometimes return the merchandise if it hadn't sold. Why would he pay the full wholesale price immediately if he could have six months' credit buying from his usual suppliers? The only way he would pay for the ring immediately was if he could purchase it at a substantial discount. That was the reason for the $450 offer.

In the end the young man decided not to sell the ring. Unhappy, he put it back in the little blue jewelry box and stood up to leave. He looked at the owner and told him that buying jewelry on the retail level was a very bad investment. With that he turned and walked out of the store.

Clearly the problem with buying jewelry at the retail level is that you have to pay retail prices. The problem with retail prices is that they are at least twice as expensive as wholesale prices. When it comes to high ticket items like jewelry, that is a very big difference.

Diamonds, precious metals, and the objects of adornment made from these valuable materials are investments for jewelers and merchants who earn their livelihood buying and reselling this merchandise for a profit. They never pay retail prices because they would not be able to resell the goods and make a profit. They buy wholesale and sell retail.

The major reason for the enormous price differential between wholesale and retail is *overhead*. Roughly defined, overhead expenses are all the general costs that are incurred in order to own and operate a business. For example, rent, salaries and benefits, bank interest, federal, state, county, and city taxes, advertisements, furniture and decorations, insurance, security alarm systems, accountants' fees, lawyers' fees, and government license fees are overhead expenses.

Overhead expenses do not include the cost of the jewelry inventory that the store purchases for resale. Therefore, retail overhead expenses are all those costs that are not directly related to the wholesale price of the jewelry. They are extra expenses that consumers will have to pay for but that they cannot wear out of the store. In my opinion, those overhead dollars would be better spent on larger or better quality jewelry than spent on the maintenance of someone else's business.

It is very costly to open and operate a retail jewelry store. The national chains, department stores, regional chains, and the finer independent stores like to be located in the fashionable and protected shopping malls where there are many different types of retail merchants and the parking is abundant. The atmosphere is conducive for shopping but the rents at these malls are extremely expensive.

Furnishing a retail jewelry store is very costly. The floor and wall showcases, interior partitions for offices and work space, carpets, lighting, vault, and security system can easily cost hundreds of thousands of dollars depending on the degree of elaborateness.

Another costly weekly expense is the salary of the manager

or owner and his staff. In the better malls the hours are long and most retailers require additional staff or perhaps two separate shifts.

The point is that somebody has to pay for all these overhead expenses if the business is going to make money and continue. It is the customers who pay the expenses and profit by purchasing at that store. **The question is, do you really want to pay 200 percent to 400 percent above the wholesale price for the privilege of shopping at a fashionable shopping mall, in an attractively decorated jewelry store, served by a salesperson who presents the merchandise in a pleasing manner and wraps your purchase in a fancy little box?**

There are people who insist on purchasing at prestigious retail stores because they believe that is the only way to obtain quality merchandise. This is part of the "you get what you pay for" mentality which mistakenly assumes that it is necessary to pay top dollar in order to obtain superior products. This book will dramatically demonstrate that you do not have to pay excessive prices to acquire fine jewelry.

Some customers buy fine jewelry at exclusive retail stores so they have the right to say that they do their shopping at very expensive places. If having the bragging rights to shopping at high-priced stores is meaningful to you, then my book will painfully point out the cost of this type of psychological indulgence.

Personally, I have always tried to purchase as inexpensively as possible, regardless of the item. I never cared where I bought a car, a television set, or an item of clothing as long as I legally obtained the quality or brand I was after at an inexpensive price. The important part was having and using the merchandise I purchased, not the box it was wrapped in, or the name of the store it came from. If the quality and the price were the same, wouldn't you rather have a two-carat diamond engagement ring from a wholesaler who has a small showroom in a nondescript office building than a one-carat diamond that came from the most prestigious jeweler in town? Once you take the ring out of the fancy little box and place it on your finger, no one will ever know or care where the ring was purchased, but the size and quality of the diamond will be apparent forever.

A relatively small group of buyers are so wealthy that they really don't care how much money they spend. I would be amazed if those individuals will bother to read this book. If they do read this book, however, I think they will be surprised and disturbed to discover that for the same number of dollars spent, a far more spectacular piece of fine jewelry can be purchased.

Most people purchase fine jewelry at the retail level because they don't know how else to buy. They are so accustomed to walking into a store, or ordering through a catalog or by television, that they mistakenly believe that these are the only ways to acquire fine jewelry. This book will simply and easily show the average consumer how to purchase fine jewelry at wholesale prices.

I have a friend who refuses to buy fine jewelry because he claims he does not understand what he is buying. "How do I know that the bracelet is really gold and not brass that is gold-plated? How do I know the diamond is real and not a good imitation? How do I know that I am getting the quality the jeweler promised?" he will ask me. After reading this book the consumers will have the knowledge to determine whether what they are purchasing is what it is represented to be.

I decided to write this book on how to properly purchase jewelry because I believe there is a tremendous need for it. Given my years of experience in the jewelry business I know that there are millions of consumers who regularly pay more for their fine jewelry purchases than they have to. In addition, the average consumer of commercial jewelry today does not receive as high quality merchandise as is generally advertised.

For the general public, jewelry is not an investment but

ornaments to be worn and enjoyed. That is the unwritten rule of the jewelry industry unless a consumer is able to buy on the wholesale level. After reading *How to Buy Jewelry Wholesale* the average shopper is going to know how to break the rule and buy at the right price.

Therefore, the purposes of this book are to:

1. Give the readers a rudimentary knowledge of diamonds, gold, silver, and platinum jewelry so they will be able to purchase intelligently;

2. Teach the readers how to locate and utilize accredited experts to determine the true quality and value of jewelry they are considering purchasing;

3. Provide reference and source information that will enable the readers to accurately determine the current wholesale price of the jewelry they are considering purchasing;

4. Reveal where and how to actually purchase jewelry at true wholesale prices.

The scope of this book is limited to loose diamonds; fine jewelry that contains diamonds set in either gold or platinum, including engagement rings and wedding sets; and gold, platinum, and sterling silver jewelry without diamonds. The reason for this limited scope is twofold:

1. These categories of jewelry are by far the most commonly purchased items, accounting for nearly 70 percent of all jewelry purchases in North America in 1996;

2. Diamonds, gold, platinum, and silver have structured, international markets. The current market price for platinum, gold, and silver may be obtained anywhere in the world, twenty-four hours a day. The prices are readily available from newspapers, brokerage houses, coin and gold dealers, precious metal refineries, and banks. Diamonds are traded daily in organized

exchanges (bourses) around the world and the wholesale selling prices are monitored.

I have purposely omitted pearls and colored stone jewelry from this book because they do not enjoy the stability and liquidity of a structured market. It is extremely difficult for the average consumer to successfully purchase or sell colored stone or pearl jewelry due to the variety and complexity of the subject and the lack of wholesale pricing information. Unlike fine jewelry made from diamonds, gold, platinum, and silver, where standard and reasonable prices can be calculated, the pearl and colored stone business is infested with deceptive, quality-enhanced merchandise that is sold to the unwary consumer at very large profit margins.

I hope you enjoy reading this book and profit from the experience. If after reading this book you have additional questions on how to purchase specific items, or believe that you have been ripped off and would like to tell your story, please write to me. My mailing address is:

Frank J. Adler
P.O. Box 611802
Miami, Florida 33621

My e-mail address on the Internet is:

FAROWER@AOL.COM

CHAPTER 1

The Marketplace

Jewelry is considered a blind item because it is difficult for the average consumer to see and appreciate differences in quality and size. To the ordinary person a flawless diamond might appear no different than one of far lesser quality. A one-carat diamond might look the same in size as a diamond a quarter carat larger or smaller. A bracelet might have the color associated with 18-karat yellow gold but in fact be made from 10-karat gold. Unless you are an expert, the differences in colored stones, diamonds, and gold are so subtle that they are very difficult to detect. Few members of the general public have enough knowledge to make an intelligent decision when purchasing a diamond or a piece of fine jewelry. In the past, these unknowing consumers depended on a retailer to guide them in a fair and honest manner.

This arrangement of forced trust between the buyer and seller of fine jewelry has always struck me as a questionable arrangement. The sellers cannot be fair and impartial because they have a vested interest in the outcome of the transaction, namely to make a profitable sale. Over the years I have observed a number of variations on this theme, none of which, in my opinion, were satisfactory.

Obviously, the best arrangement possible between the retailer and the buyer is that the seller tells the truth with respect to the quality and size of the merchandise. Most of your better retail stores, to one degree or another, follow this policy when representing their merchandise. The problem is that the consumer will generally pay an exorbitant price for this honesty.

At the other end of the spectrum, the retailer may offer discounted prices on his merchandise, but the goods are not the quality or size that they are represented to be. If a diamond, for example, is sold as a half-carat stone (50 points) and in reality it weighs less, then the consumer is actually paying a considerably higher price for that diamond. This type of deception occurs all too frequently to trusting, unenlightened consumers of fine jewelry.

The question of where to purchase jewelry is directly related to how knowledgeable you are. The less informed you are, the more reliant you are upon the traditional retail distribution network. At this level the purchaser has to depend on the integrity of the retailer, a very unenviable position to be in.

Once consumers become educated and understand how the values of fine jewelry and diamonds are determined, they will shy away from the traditional retailers and begin purchasing from entirely different sources. If, for whatever reason, they continue to use traditional retail outlets, their buying approach will dramatically change based on their newly acquired knowledge and confidence.

The most widely used retail outlet in our society is the store. From a very early age, most people are psychologically conditioned to go to the store to buy whatever is needed or wanted. Therefore it comes as no surprise that most people go to a jewelry store to purchase jewelry. According to the Jewelers Board of Trade, there are more than 44,000 retail jewelry stores operating in the United States today.

The kindest comment I can make about the vast majority of retail jewelry stores is that they are good showrooms. A store will prominently display merchandise in its windows as well as in interior showcases. Many stores, particularly those located in shopping malls, go to great lengths and expense to tastefully decorate their premises. Consequently, due to the universal appeal of jewelry and the pleasant atmosphere, retail jewelry stores are very popular places to browse.

If you are considering a jewelry purchase, but do not know exactly what you want, a good place to start is the retail jewelry stores. You can see a large selection of the newest styles of merchandise available and learn about the items. If, for example, you are interested in purchasing a gold chain, you can see the many different styles and lengths that are available. You can try on the chains to determine what length is desirable, as well as see how the chains lie on your neck. You can ask the salesperson basic questions such as whether the chain is hollow or solid, how well it wears, if it breaks easily, what karat gold was used, and the weight of the gold in grams. The salesperson may or may not have all this information. If the store has a repair department, you can ask the repair jeweler which chains have the fewest repairs, or if the chain you are thinking of buying breaks or kinks easily.

If you are considering a diamond purchase and find pieces that you like, you should ask the size of the diamonds used, what quality of diamonds were used, the total diamond weight, and if there is a report from an accredited gemological laboratory describing the quality of the diamonds used in the piece of jewelry.

Visit a number of retail stores and compare merchandise until you determine precisely what you want to purchase. If, for example, you want to buy a gold chain you should decide what style, length, weight, karat, and price you want prior to approaching a wholesaler. If you are in the market to purchase a diamond you should determine what size, shape, color grade, clarity grade, and price you want prior to searching for a diamond dealer to buy from.

Personally, I would never buy jewelry from a retail store. The overwhelming reason is that the selling price of the jewelry is too high. A single-unit, mom-and-pop-type operation will mark up the price of the jewelry by a minimum of 100 percent because of costly overhead expenses such as rent, salaries, advertising, cost

of inventory, taxes, and, of course, profit. The markup in department and chain stores will probably be even higher.

Another disadvantage of retail stores is that they are forced
to purchase merchandise that falls into popular price ranges due
to their high overhead expenses and the pressure exerted by the
competition. For example, a retail chain knows that 14-karat
hollow gold hoop earrings they sell to the consumer for $39.95
are very popular. To sell at that price the chain must purchase
the merchandise for $20.00 wholesale at the very most because
the business requires a minimum of a 100 percent markup to
make a small profit. This type of pressure buying does not guarantee good-quality merchandise because the emphasis is on
price, not quality. As the retailer's overhead expenses climb, or
the cost of raw materials (e.g. gold) increases, or manufacturers'
costs increase, the quality of the merchandise will have to
decrease if retail prices are to be maintained. It is for these reasons that the merchandise offered by retailers today is of such
poor quality. Gold jewelry items such as earrings, chains, and
bracelets are constantly becoming lighter and flimsier, and are
subject to far more breakage than merchandise that is built with
greater structural integrity. The diamonds that are offered at
popular retail prices are getting smaller in size and the quality of
these stones is decreasing rapidly.

The other disadvantage associated with retail stores is that,
with few exceptions, the salespeople are not jewelry professionals. They are usually sales clerks who simply read the information on the ticket attached to the merchandise and are able
to answer only the most elementary questions. I prefer to deal
with professionals who are experts in the commodities in which
they are dealing. These professionals are normally found only on
the wholesale level.

The major difference between a retail jewelry store and a
department store is that a retail jewelry store depends solely on
jewelry, watches, and repairs for its existence while a department

store has many other types of merchandise. The jewelry division is very important to most department stores because it is the unit that normally generates the most gross profit. The reason for this is that a piece of jewelry such as an engagement ring is difficult to compare to another ring very similar to it. For example, if a consumer is in the market for a particular brand name and model color television it is easy to go price shopping. The consumer knows the model will be exactly the same regardless of where the television is purchased. The only variables are who will sell it at the lowest price and the terms of the warranty. The same type of comparison is impossible with jewelry items because there are no brand names and each item is different; there are no comparable standards.

Regardless of misleading advertisements placed in the media and the 50-percent-off sales they promote, there are no bargains to be had in the jewelry sections of department stores. Remember, 50 percent off a jewelry item that is marked up 200 percent to 400 percent is not a bargain, it's just a high retail price!

A very American phenomenon is catalog shopping. In the 1800s, when this country was expanding westward, most of the pioneers living in remote areas depended on catalogs for many items. For these adventurous settlers, the catalog was a link to civilization as well as a graphic illustration of the latest fashions and gadgetry. In fact, one of the largest retailers in the country, Sears Roebuck and Company, was built on catalog sales. To this day billions of dollars of merchandise are still sold through catalogs.

There are probably many items that can be bought inexpensively and with confidence through catalogs. Unfortunately jewelry is not one of them. One of the problems with buying jewelry from a picture is that you will not really know what you are purchasing until the merchandise arrives. In most instances the catalog description of a piece of jewelry is deliberately vague, not giving a great deal of specific information on the quality of the diamond(s) or the metal weight of the jewelry. Without specific information it is impossible to judge whether or not the item offered is a good deal. In addition, it is very difficult for the average consumer to visualize what the item will really look like because the catalog photographs of the jewelry are so greatly enlarged and enhanced.

Catalog house prices may be less expensive than most retail jewelry or department stores but they are still retail prices. The cost of purchasing merchandise from wholesalers and manufacturers, the cost of producing, printing and mailing thousands of catalogs, and the normal overhead expenses involved with running a catalog operation must be recovered by including them plus a profit in the prices of the merchandise sold. Unless you live in an extremely remote area, buying jewelry sight unseen, without a highly accurate description or an accompanying accredited grading report, is a very bad idea.

There are two distinct types of discounters in the jewelry business: the ones that really give a significant discount from retail prices and the ones that pretend to give a discount. There are two factors that determine whether or not a merchant can be categorized as a true discounter.

The first and most important factor is the amount of overhead the business has. All of the true discounters I have seen have relatively low overheads. Many times the business is located in an office building, occupying one or more offices to save on rent. Generally the decorations are modest and functional, and the owner is on the premises working with a small, knowledgeable staff. Many times the staff is composed of family members, making the entire effort a family business. In this type of sparse environment, where expenses are kept to a bare minimum, and the purchasing or manufacture of merchandise is expertly done, you may obtain prices that are significantly below the retail level.

The second factor is the honest desire on the part of the merchant or jeweler to sell at discounted prices. In a number of cases a business will establish the impression of being a discounter but in fact have prices as high as any other retail establishment. This is particularly true of pawnshops. They like to give the impression that they have purchased merchandise below the market price and so are able and willing to sell the same merchandise below retail price. In truth, however, these shrewd merchants make a very good living by being experts on the wholesale and retail value of many different kinds of merchandise. They normally buy cheap but sell expensive and they conduct their businesses in a low overhead environment. That's why there are few bankruptcies among pawnbrokers.

Vendors that conduct their businesses at flea markets also like to give the impression that they sell jewelry at discounted prices. These merchants purchase their merchandise from many of the same suppliers that traditional retail jewelers buy from, but they normally pay higher wholesale prices. The reason for this difference in pricing is that most flea market jewelers do not have the same degree of financial stability, volume and type of purchases, or credit worthiness as their traditional retail counterparts.

Most flea market vendors do almost all of their business on weekends. Having far less time to make sales, these vendors normally have fewer unit sales per week than their traditional retail counterparts. This means that each sale a merchant makes at a flea market is important and those fewer collective sales have to generate enough revenue to pay the overhead expenses as well as make a profit. It is important to remember that for many vendors the flea market is a full-time occupation and their livelihood depends on sales that are generated from this business.

Lastly, flea market jewelers normally don't sell expensive pieces of jewelry where the dollar amount of profit is significant. Consumers in the market to purchase a large diamond or an important piece of jewelry generally don't make that type of purchase at a flea market. Consequently, flea market jewelers sell relatively inexpensive jewelry such as lightweight chains, earrings, charms, and rings where the profit in dollar amounts per item is not great. For example, a chain that is marked up 100 percent and sells for $50 will yield a $25 profit in real dollars. Even though the profit is high in percentage terms, think about the number of chain sales needed to make enough money to pay expenses. Unless a vendor is selling many items per day it is necessary to charge high prices in order to make enough money to pay expenses and make a living.

The only way you will know for sure whether or not you are receiving a substantial savings from retail prices is to be able to analyze the piece of jewelry and determine what its wholesale price should be. After reading this book, you should be able to make this wholesale pricing determination or know what sources to contact to gain this vital information.

The modern-day equivalent of sales by catalog is the advent of television home shopping networks. This relatively new method of retail distribution utilizes an entire cable channel that is allocated primarily to the sale of assorted merchandise. During the programming day and evening the merchandise is offered by various hosts in a show or infomercial format. Typically the viewer sees an item that he or she would like to purchase, telephones the home shopping network's free 800 number, and orders by using a credit card, mailing in a check, or receiving the merchandise on a cash on delivery (COD) basis.

Even though television home shopping can be very convenient and entertaining, I would not recommend buying jewelry this way. The problem is that the viewer is being asked to purchase jewelry without having the information to analyze what the item is really worth. For example, the network host shows a shiny gold chain and says, "This lovely 14-karat gold chain is 16 inches in length, and is only $99." At this point the viewer does not know the most important factor in analyzing the value of the chain, namely the weight of the chain. In addition, the viewer doesn't know whether the chain is solid or hollow, imported or manufactured domestically, or what the design or finish actually looks like. In my opinion buying jewelry from an image on a television screen is similar to buying from a catalog, and to me that is the same as buying sight unseen, which is totally unacceptable.

Furthermore, I haven't seen any real bargains on any of the television shopping networks. The overhead costs associated with selling merchandise via television are certainly not inexpensive. To begin with, the shopping network has to buy merchandise from manufacturers and wholesalers. Then there is the cost of the cable network, producing the show, answering the tens of thousands of telephone calls, shipping the merchandise, administrative costs, rents, benefits, and a hundred other sundry expenses involved in running a successful television marketing organization. Finally, the company needs to make a profit and pay dividends to its stockholders. All factors considered, the expenses involved in a successful television home shopping operation may be as high as a large retail operation. Therefore, the prices asked for jewelry will be retail prices. The only real difference is that you can shop from the comfort and convenience of your home. In my opinion, the prices for jewelry offered by television home shopping networks are too high for the privilege of being a couch potato consumer.

Even though the home shopping networks can generate volume sales, they do not normally receive rock-bottom wholesale prices from their suppliers. The reason is that like all mass merchandisers, they are very difficult customers. They demand a number of services from their suppliers that are both costly and troublesome.

First, the networks require credit, and this causes two major problems. The interest cost of the money for giving 60-, 90-, or 120-day credit terms is paid by the wholesaler. Next and even more problematic is the fluctuation in material prices, such as gold. For example, you are an importer of gold chains and you sell to a network with 90-day credit terms. What if the price of gold goes up significantly before you are paid? In that case you could actually lose money on the deal, because when you replace the merchandise it might cost you more than you sold it for. If you want to hedge the price of gold, which means eliminating this gamble by guaranteeing the future price of gold on the commodities market, it will cost at least 1 percent of the total amount of the sale. If you are working on a very small profit margin, as most wholesalers are, this insurance will be prohibitively expensive.

Second, all mass merchandisers demand the right to return goods for full credit. This right to return unsold or damaged merchandise can be disastrous. A sale in this case isn't really a sale, but is actually a consignment. This arrangement has caused a number of bankruptcies because the supplier is expecting to be paid and actually ends up with returned, possibly damaged and unsalable merchandise. In order to avoid these severe problems, the suppliers need to charge a higher per unit price for their goods. Unless the wholesaler or manufacturer can charge the network for the privilege of borrowing money and returning unsold merchandise, the supplier stands a good chance of losing money.

Now ask yourself, who would wholesalers rather deal with, a customer whose demands are so difficult that the wholesalers never know if they are going to break even, let alone make a profit, or a customer like you, who buys a piece of jewelry, pays for it immediately, and does not return it? I think the answer is obvious, and that is why you can buy wholesale as long as you know what you are doing!

Having spent a considerable amount of time examining traditional retail distributors, it is now time to reveal from which sources jewelry should be purchased. In my opinion, the only way to purchase diamonds and fine jewelry at wholesale prices is to purchase from wholesalers, importers, and manufacturers. These are the same sources that retail jewelers use.

Merchants who sell diamonds on a wholesale basis are called *diamond dealers*. These diamond experts either cut and polish the gems themselves, or purchase loose, cut (finished) diamonds from other foreign or domestic cutters, or combine both activities. These merchants normally inventory large stocks of loose diamonds for the purpose of resale. They also work with other diamond dealers either directly or through diamond clubs (bourses) to buy or sell diamonds.

If you are in the market to purchase a diamond it is preferable to buy from a reputable diamond dealer. The following chapters will describe in great detail the information necessary to purchase a diamond with confidence.

Fine jewelry can be purchased from a number of different sources on the wholesale level. Jewelry manufacturers, casters, findings houses, and importers of gold and silver jewelry are among the various suppliers that make, import, inventory, and sell jewelry wholesale.

There are thousands of fine jewelry manufacturers in the United States and Canada. They fabricate every conceivable jewelry item including chains, rings, bracelets, earrings, pendants, and charms in gold, silver, and platinum.

Precious metal casters are manufacturers who produce jewelry in a partially completed state. The items are reproduced from wax patterns into precious metal (e.g. gold, silver, or platinum). The castings are in an unfinished condition and will require additional work. These finishing processes generally are not performed by the caster but by other craftsmen such as jewelers, stone setters, and polishers. The advantage of buying from a caster, and then subcontracting the remaining work to independent craftsmen, is that this is normally the least expensive way to have a piece of solid, casted fine jewelry made.

Findings houses traditionally carry a wide assortment of parts used in the manufacture of fine jewelry. They purchase these different items in large quantities from findings manufacturers and normally resell the merchandise to small jewelry manufacturers, retail stores, repair shops, and diamond and colored stone dealers in much smaller quantities. They function as a convenient warehouse to many businesses that order in small quantities. Among the items that these businesses sell are die-stamped rings, earrings, and pendants. Most larger findings houses produce illustrated catalogs. Upon request these businesses will normally mail their latest catalog to a potential customer. Findings houses may be an excellent source from which to purchase certain standard jewelry items, such as die-struck, four-prong engagement rings or die-struck stud earrings at wholesale prices.

The largest variety of foreign precious metal jewelry may be found in the showrooms of *gold and silver jewelry importers*. These merchants purchase various jewelry items such as chains, earrings, bracelets, pendants, rings, and charms from manufacturers in various countries around the world, primarily Italy, Israel, Spain, and the Far East.

Most of the imported jewelry available through traditional retail sources is purchased from these importers. The importers normally purchase and sell the fine jewelry by weight (see Chapter 16). They pay for the amount of precious metal used in the piece of jewelry plus a surcharge for machine time and labor. As a rule of thumb, most precious metal merchandise, especially imported or machine-made goods, should be purchased by weight. This is the standard wholesale method of doing business for this type of jewelry.

One of the truly phenomenal developments of the electronic information age is the *Internet*. This voluntary linking of thousands of separate computer networks offers a gigantic worldwide forum in which to share all types of information as well as establish a new distribution system for the sale of goods and services.

It is my opinion that, for the informed consumer, the Internet is the best source for purchasing diamonds and fine jewelry at wholesale prices. Individual businesses are presently able to effectively reach millions of potential consumers at very low costs. They are able to list on individual web sites or in Internet shopping malls all the pertinent information needed to determine the wholesale price of a diamond, or a piece of fine jewelry. All of the jewelry web sites have corresponding e-mail addresses that you can use to ask very specific questions about the diamond or precious metal jewelry you are considering. This two-way dialogue will allow an informed consumer to gather all the relevant facts prior to making a decision. This dialogue is not possible on television home shopping networks or through catalog shopping. This will allow an educated consumer to determine the value of jewelry offered. With this low-overhead, mass-communication system in place, diamond merchants and jewelry manufacturers are able to bypass the traditional retail distribution system (stores, catalogs, television home shopping) and offer their merchandise directly at wholesale prices. What is needed at this time to make the Internet the most effective mass-marketing tool of all time is to have more subscribers on the net and have a safe system for making payment by credit card. These developments, although not in place at this time, will become available soon.

Having discussed where you should and shouldn't go to purchase a piece of jewelry, the remainder of this book will be dedicated to explaining how you can purchase intelligently from reputable wholesale sources.

CHAPTER 2

The Diamond Engagement Ring

The diamond engagement ring is the most significant jewelry purchase many people will ever make. Ideally it is meant to be a symbolic representation of a romantic commitment that is intended to last a lifetime. In reality, it is the largest single source of profit that the jewelry industry has available.

Each year tens of millions of dollars are spent on promoting the romantic aspects of diamond engagement rings. De Beers, the worldwide diamond syndicate, proclaims that "diamonds are forever." In advertisements that appear around the world starry-eyed young couples are depicted holding hands as they look longingly at a diamond engagement ring. The jewelry industry has done everything in its power to promote the concept that a diamond engagement ring is the ultimate symbol of love and betrothal.

Currently the largest consuming nation of diamond engagement rings is the United States, followed very closely by Japan. The irony in this statistic is that the diamond engagement ring was not part of the Japanese culture prior to 1945. Only after the war ended, and hundreds of millions of dollars were spent to promote the romanticism of the diamond engagement ring, did the Japanese begin to purchase them. Today 80 percent of Japan's brides receive diamond engagement rings prior to marriage.

Unfortunately, despite all this advertisement, most people do not have enough knowledge to purchase an engagement ring intelligently. They are generally caught up in the moment, in an excited, euphoric state where their involvement with each other makes them vulnerable to the powerful marketing of the jewelry industry. It is at this moment that most couples buy the wrong engagement ring, for the wrong price, and for all the wrong reasons. It is my sincere hope that the remainder of this book will teach you what factors are important to consider when purchasing an engagement ring, or any other piece of fine jewelry. After careful reading you will know how to determine the quality of a diamond, what the wholesale prices of the diamond and ring should be, and how to go about purchasing the item you desire at the best possible price.

Please don't misunderstand my purpose and motivation for writing this book. I am not trying to take the romance out of purchasing a diamond engagement ring or wedding rings. Quite the contrary, I am trying to make the experience more pleasant and less frightening because I want you to be armed with all the facts and knowledge necessary to buy exactly what you want at the best possible price. I also want you to be assured that you have not been cheated, that you have received the size and quality diamond and precious metal jewelry that you have paid for.

By properly using the information contained in this book you will save money when you purchase your diamond engagement ring. With the savings you may buy either a larger or better quality stone for the same number of dollars, or you may use your extra money for a more exotic or longer honeymoon, extra dinners at pleasant restaurants, a larger wedding celebration, or anything else your heart desires. The point is that you will have more options available because you will be able to purchase more wisely and have more money available.

There are normally two components that make up a diamond engagement ring: the diamond(s) and the ring. I know this sounds ridiculously simple, but you would be surprised how many people don't realize that the diamond(s) part of this combination is where 95 percent of the value is and the ring is a comparatively minor expenditure. The reason I bring this up is that many times the woman who is about to receive an engagement ring is more concerned with the style and appearance of the overall ring than about the size, quality, and price of the diamond(s). Remember that this is an emotionally charged, once-in-a-lifetime experience, fueled by misleading advertising that lends itself to buying an engagement ring for the wrong set of criteria. Buying style as opposed to value, purchasing a meaningless brand or famous store name, or being swayed by alluring and romantic advertisements are the wrong reasons for selecting an engagement ring. Therefore, the best approach to purchasing a diamond engagement ring is to decide on the style of the ring first but to purchase the diamond(s) separately. For example, you have shopped the various retail stores in your area and you have decided that you want to purchase a 14-karat yellow gold solitaire ring with a center diamond of one carat and two side baguette diamonds weighing 15 points each. My recommendation would be to purchase the diamonds from a diamond wholesaler and then to purchase the ring from a manufacturing jeweler, a findings house, a caster, or a discount retailer. The best way to purchase an engagement ring is to buy the diamond(s) first because this is where most of the value is. An engagement ring is like a painting: the diamond is the art and the ring is only the frame. I would not purchase a ring already set with the diamond(s) because it is the more expensive way of buying and you really can't determine what size or quality you are actually purchasing unless you remove the stones and examine them.

Below you will find a list of things *not to do* when purchasing a diamond engagement ring. I strongly suggest that you use it as a checklist when shopping. At first reading, not all the points will be totally clear, but after you have read the appropriate chapters they will make perfect sense. My suggestion is to quickly read through this list and then reread it before you actually go out to make your purchase.

1. Don't start to shop for a diamond engagement ring until you firmly establish how much money you can reasonably afford to spend;

2. Don't purchase jewelry in a retail store unless the store is willing to sell at wholesale or discounted prices;

3. Don't buy an engagement ring with the diamond(s) already set;

4. Don't blindly accept the traditional jeweler's four "C"s value for diamonds until you understand what carat, color, clarity, and cut really mean;

5. Don't buy a fancy-shaped diamond when you can purchase a round, brilliant-cut stone;

6. Don't buy a diamond over half a carat without a GIA Diamond Report;

7. Don't buy a diamond unless you have seen the Rapaport wholesale diamond price list;

8. Don't buy a diamond until you have its quality verified by an independent, reputable expert;

9. Don't be mislead by exaggerated or fallacious advertisements;

10. Don't be mislead by brand or famous names attached to jewelry merchandise. Brand or designer names mean absolutely nothing in the jewelry business because each diamond or precious metal piece needs to be analyzed individually. Don't be fooled or mesmerized because some salesperson says, "This is a (name of a famous store) diamond."

11. Don't insure your engagement ring without using a GIA Diamond Report as the basis of proof of quality;

12. Don't buy from any business that does not disclose the weight of an item made in precious metal;

13. Don't buy an engagement ring until you calculate its intrinsic precious metal value and determine the amount you are being charged above intrinsic value.

CHAPTER 3

Diamonds: An Overview

It takes years of practice, viewing thousands of different stones, to become truly proficient at grading the quality of a diamond. To expect a layperson to become a diamond expert just by reading a chapter or two is totally unreasonable. This section will introduce the different factors that determine the quality of a diamond. By having an overview of diamond grading considerations, you will be better able to determine what shape, size, and quality diamond you want to buy. In the following chapters you will learn what questions to ask while selecting a stone, and how to best utilize the expertise of an impartial registered gemologist or appraiser. Also, you will learn how to read and understand the results of a diamond grading report issued by an accredited gemological laboratory.

WHAT KIND OF DIAMOND DO YOU WANT TO BUY?

This may seem like a strange question, but it is the logical place to start the search for a diamond. The first thing you should do is ask yourself the following questions:

1. WHY ARE YOU PURCHASING THIS DIAMOND?

Most gem-grade diamonds are purchased to be worn as ornaments in some type of fine jewelry. It may be used as a symbol of love as in an engagement, wedding, anniversary, birthday, or graduation present. These diamonds differ in quality from investment-grade stones, which are not normally used in commercial jewelry. Gem-grade diamonds usually have a trace of yellow or brown body color and possess internal and external imperfections. Fortunately, most of these characteristics seldom have any real effect on the beauty and liveliness of the diamond.

Investment-grade gems, because of their whiteness or lack of color, and absence of various internal and external flaws and blemishes, are extremely rare, but they are not necessarily more beautiful than the diamonds used in commercial jewelry.

2. HOW MUCH MONEY CAN YOU AFFORD TO SPEND ON A DIAMOND?

The search for a diamond should begin only after you decide how much money you can reasonably afford to spend. It is a waste of time to look at a $5,000 diamond if you are limited to spending $2,500. The traditional rule of thumb is to spend two months of your gross salary on an engagement ring. For example, if you earn $600 per week then you could spend up to $4,800 for the diamond and the ring.

3. WHICH SHAPE OF DIAMOND DO YOU PREFER?

Diamonds are cut into numerous different shapes that include round, marquise, pear, oval, heart, and emerald cut. You should determine which of these shapes the recipient prefers. My overwhelming professional preference is for round, brilliant-cut diamonds because they display the greatest amount of brilliance and fire, are easiest to grade and categorize, and are normally quickly resold.

4. WHAT SIZE DIAMOND DO YOU PREFER?

Diamonds are available in different sizes. In many cases you will have to choose between a larger stone of lesser quality or a smaller stone of better quality. This choice is a matter of personal preference.

5. WHAT COLOR GRADE DO YOU WANT?

The whiter or more colorless a diamond is, the *rarer* and more expensive that stone will be. In jewelry, due to the subtle change in color from one grade to the next, the finest color grades are not necessary. This is an area where quality can be sacrificed without any noticeable difference in the beauty of the stone. In my experience, diamonds that have a tinge of body color are more dazzling than their cold, icy-looking, colorless counterparts.

6. WHAT CLARITY GRADE DO YOU WANT?

Polished diamonds are examined to determine their imperfections by magnifying them ten times their actual size. The instrument used for this purpose is called a *loupe*. The diamonds with the least number of internal and external flaws and blemishes receive the highest grades for clarity. Unless a flaw or blemish is a major fault, one that can be seen with the naked eye or one that might cause the diamond to break, these minor imperfections have little or no effect on the beauty or personality of the diamond. These clarity grades only signify the *rarity* of the stone. Therefore, you can purchase a diamond of a lesser clarity grade and still have a beautiful diamond. Remember, most imperfections that affect clarity grades can only be seen with the aid of a ten-power magnifier. Who, besides a jeweler, is going to examine a ring that closely?

7. IS THE DIAMOND WELL PROPORTIONED?

This is the most important factor in determining the beauty of a diamond. If the diamond is poorly cut the stone can look dull, lifeless, oily, or larger or smaller than it is supposed to look.

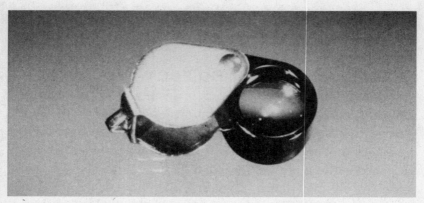

A Ten-Power Loupe. Photograph courtesy of © GIA
(Gemological Institute of America)

This is the one area that should not be sacrificed when choosing a diamond. Ironically, this critical area of "cut" or "make" of a diamond is the least emphasized by the jewelry industry because of a combination of ignorance on the retail level and the diamond cutters' desire to cut stones for weight retention and additional profits. For example, a cutter owns a rough diamond that weighs 3.00 carats and costs $1,500. If this stone is cut to correct portions, it will yield a 1.50-carat finished diamond that the cutter can sell for $5,000. Using inferior proportions, the cutter can manufacture a 2.00-carat diamond from the same rough stone that will sell for $5,700 because of its larger, more desirable size. The 2.00-carat diamond, because of its improper proportioning, will not have nearly as much fire or brilliance as the smaller stone, but you can guess which stone will be manufactured.

8. DOES A DIAMOND GRADING REPORT COME WITH THE DIAMOND?

Any diamond over a half carat (.50 carat) should be accompanied by a grading report from the Gemological Institute of

America. This report will identify the stone and give a professional, unbiased opinion with regard to the size, shape, clarity, color, and proportions of the gem. The information contained in this report is extremely useful when purchasing a stone because it authenticates the quality and characteristics of the diamond. It is also an extremely important validating document when insuring the diamond against loss or theft.

It is imperative that you verify that the diamond grading report matches the diamond you are considering purchasing. It has happened that unscrupulous merchants present a favorable diamond grading report that was not issued for the stone they are attempting to sell. It has also happened that counterfeit diamond grading reports have been used to make a sale. I will explain in Chapter 11 how to avoid both types of fraud.

To answer most of the above questions intelligently you need to understand how diamonds are **really** graded and which factors are **most** important in the selection of a stone. Traditionally, jewelers like to point to the color, clarity, and carat weight of a diamond as being the most significant factors. Actually, the characteristic jewelers talk least about, namely the cut or make of the stone, is by far the most important consideration. The factors that determine the quality of the cut or manufacture of a diamond are fully explored in Chapter 7.

CHAPTER 4

Carat Weight

When I lived in Montreal, Canada, I had a friend who planned to get engaged. The couple had visited a number of jewelry stores and the girlfriend had her heart set on a one-carat, round diamond engagement ring. The problem was that my friend was on a very tight budget and didn't have enough money to buy his girlfriend the size diamond she wanted. One day he came to my office for help. After determining exactly how much money he was able to spend I showed him a diamond that he could afford. The stone had the physical size of a one-carat diamond (6.50 mm in diameter) but only weighed 91 points or .91 carat. This is

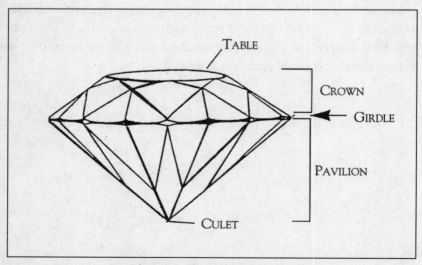

Parts of a Faceted Diamond

a less desirable weight than a one-carat stone or larger, so it was considerably less expensive. When a diamond appears considerably larger than its actual weight, it is called a spread stone. The problem with this type of cut or make is that the proportions of the stone allow light to leak out of the bottom of the stone (pavilion) instead of reflecting back through the top of the diamond (crown). The result is a loss of fire and brilliance. However, my friend was able to stay within his budget and please his girlfriend because he made a practical compromise. He purchased a less desirable size diamond (.91 carat) that had proportions that did not display the maximum potential beauty of the stone, but did appear to be as large as a one-carat diamond. In the end everyone was pleased.

THE CARAT

The universal unit of measurement used to weigh diamonds worldwide is the metric carat. The metric carat weighs 200 milligrams, $1/5$ of a gram (5 carats equal one gram). One carat (written 1.00 carat) is further divided into points; 100 points equal one carat. If a diamond is $1/4$ carat it is also 25 points (100 points divided by 4 equals 25 points), expressed as a decimal .25 carat. A $1/2$-carat stone would weigh 50 points (100 points divided by 2 equals 50 points), expressed as .50 carat. The written abbreviation for carat is ct. The following chart lists the popular sizes of diamonds and how they are written and spoken.

FRACTIONAL SIZE	POINT SIZE	WRITTEN	SPOKEN
$1/100$ of a carat	1 point	.01 carat	1 point
$1/20$ of a carat	5 points	.05 carat	5 points
$1/10$ of a carat	10 points	.10 carat	10 points
$1/4$ of a carat	25 points	.25 carat	25 points
			Quarter carat

Fractional Size	Point Size	Written	Spoken
⅓ of a carat	33 points	.33 carat	33 points
			Third of a carat
½ of a carat	50 points	.50 carat	50 points
			Half carat
⅔ of a carat	66 points	.66 carat	66 points
¾ of a carat	75 points	.75 carat	75 points
One carat	100 points	1.00 carat	100 points
			One carat
Two carats	200 points	2.00 carats	200 points
			Two carats

Consequently, a diamond that is one carat and 89 points is written 1.89 carats. The number before the decimal point is the number of carats and the number to the right of the decimal point is the number of points. How many individual diamonds will be needed to make a carat using a stone that weighs .005 carat? This stone is ½ of one point. Since there are 100 points in a carat, 200 of these tiny stones are needed to weigh one carat. These diamonds are called half-pointers and they do exist.

Diamonds, like apples or steak, are sold by weight. There are different prices depending on the size or quality of the stone but the price is calculated by weight. For example, a diamond that weighs one carat (1.00 ct.) is selling for $4,000. That means the price of this stone is $4,000 a carat. How would you determine the price of a diamond that weighs 1.17 carats (one carat and seventeen points) and costs $4,000 a carat? The easiest way is to multiply 1.17 carats by $4,000 per carat which would equal $4,680 (1.17 carat × $4,000 = $4,680). If a 2.35-carat diamond is selling for $6,500 per carat, how much would the total stone cost? Again we multiply 2.35 carats by $6,500 equalling $15,275 (2.35 carats × $6,500 = $15,275). If a diamond that weighs .70 carat (70 points) sells for $2,800, how much is the price per carat? In this case we divide the selling price by the number of

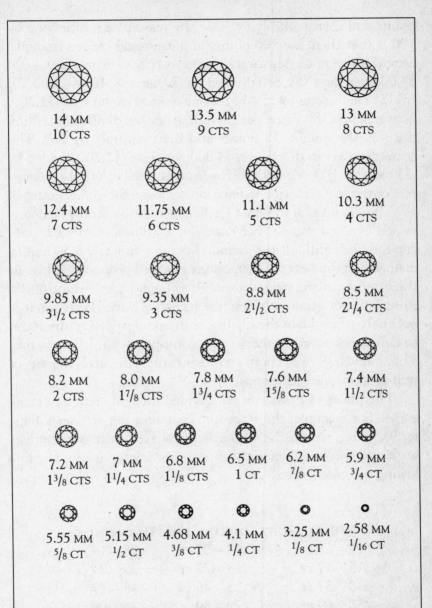

Diameters and Corresponding Weights of
Round, Brilliant-Cut Diamonds

points and then multiply by 100. The reason for multiplying by 100 is that there are 100 points in a carat and we are trying to establish the price per carat. The correct answer in this case is $4,000 per carat ($2,800 divided by .70 carat × 100 = $4,000). If a .25 carat stone (a 25 pointer or a quarter carat) costs $1,200, how much is the price per carat? Again, we divide the selling price by the number of points and then multiply by 100. The correct answer in this case is $4,800 per carat ($1,200 divided by .25 carat × 100 = $4,800). There are a number of other examples of the mathematics of diamond carat weight in Appendix B.

The question of the size of a diamond can generally be determined by carat weight. For example, a well-proportioned, one-carat, round, brilliant-cut diamond is approximately 6.50 mm in diameter. If, however, a diamond is not well proportioned, as in the example at the beginning of this chapter, the weight of the stone will not accurately describe its actual size. Therefore, it is necessary to evaluate the quality of the proportions of the stone to determine whether the weight corresponds to the ideal size. The following two charts represent the size and weight of well-proportioned diamonds.

The prices of diamonds are divided into different size categories. For example, the Rapaport Diamond Report (see Chapter 9), which reports the wholesale New York cash asking prices for loose, polished diamonds, categorizes diamonds into the following size categories:

WEIGHT CATEGORIES FOR DIAMONDS

.01 –.03 ct	.04 –.07 ct	.08 –.14 ct
.15 –.17 ct	.18 –.22 ct	.23 –.29 ct
.30 –.37 ct	.38 –.45 ct	.46 –.49 ct
.50 –.69 ct	.70 –.89 ct	.90 –.99 ct
1.00 –1.49 ct	1.50 –1.99 ct	2.00 –2.99 ct
3.00 –3.99 ct	4.00 –4.99 ct	5.00 –5.99 ct

Weight (ct)	Emerald	Marquise	Pear	Brilliant
5				
4				
3				
2½				
2				
1½				
1¼				
1				
¾				
½				

Weights & Sizes of Various Diamond Cuts

RAPAPORT: (.70–.89 CT.): 2/7/97

	IF	VVS1	VVS2	VS1	VS2	SI1	SI2	SI3	I1	I2	I3
D	88	70	63	55	49	45	40	34	27	18	12
E	70	65	56	51	47	44	39	32	26	18	11
F	64	57	51	48	45	43	38	31	26	17	11
G	56	51	48	45	43	40	36	30	25	17	10
H	50	46	44	42	40	37	34	28	24	16	10
I	43	41	39	37	36	34	30	26	23	15	10
J	37	36	35	33	31	29	(27)	23	22	14	9
K	33	32	31	29	27	25	23	20	18	13	9
L	27	26	25	24	23	22	20	16	13	11	8
M	25	24	23	22	21	20	18	15	12	10	7

W: 53.76 = 0.00%   ✦✦✦   T: 31.50 = 0.00%

RAPAPORT (1.00–1.49 CT.): 2/7/97

	IF	VVS1	VVS2	VS1	VS2	SI1	SI2	SI3	I1	I2	I3
D	164	111	96	78	68	60	54	43	35	24	15
E	111	98	79	72	66	59	53	42	34	24	14
F	97	80	72	69	64	58	51	41	33	23	14
G	79	72	68	65	61	56	49	39	32	22	13
H	69	66	63	60	57	53	47	38	31	21	13
I	61	58	55	53	50	47	42	37	30	19	12
J	54	52	50	48	46	42	(38)	33	28	18	12
K	49	47	46	44	41	39	35	31	26	17	11
L	43	42	40	38	36	34	31	28	23	16	10
M	35	34	33	31	29	27	25	23	19	15	10

W: 79.40 = 0.00%   ✦✦✦   T: 45.17 = 0.00%

Rapaport Diamond Report

For diamonds of similar quality, the prices of diamonds escalate as the sizes increase. Again, that is the reason my friend in Canada was able to purchase the spread stone for his fiancée. The combination of the small size (.90 to .95 ct.) and the poorer proportioning of the diamond significantly lowered the price per carat of the stone. Instances of these price increases based on size are shown on the above chart.

For example, a J color (see Chapter 5) SI2 (see Chapter 6) diamond weighing .75 carat costs $2,700 per carat, whereas the identical quality diamond (J color SI2) weighing 1.50 carats costs $3,800 per carat.

Color Grading

A few years ago a friend of mine wanted to buy his wife a three-carat diamond for their twenty-fifth wedding anniversary. He wanted to set the diamond in the center of a large, yellow gold antique brooch that his wife already owned. His problem was that there were a number of stones to choose from and he didn't know which would be the best deal. As a favor, I agreed to help him select the diamond that would be most appropriate.

After carefully looking at the selection of diamonds available I chose the least expensive stone. This stone was nicely proportioned and had few internal flaws. It was, however, a fairly off-color stone, meaning that its body color was a strong shade of yellow. My friend was very surprised and probably disappointed at my selection. He diplomatically pointed out that the stone was not white. I agreed and said little more. He said he wasn't sure that a yellowish diamond would please his wife. She liked quality, and all her other diamonds were white. I said nothing, which seemed to fluster my friend. Finally, using a pair of tweezers, I picked up the stone and placed it in an opening on top of the brooch. The bright yellow gold surrounded the diamond and acted as a complementary color, thereby making the diamond appear quite a bit whiter. Next to the diamond I had chosen, I placed the whitest stone in the selection. Once again the shiny yellow gold reflected off the diamond and the white stone appeared far more yellow than was actually the case. In fact, it would be difficult for the untrained eye to distinguish which stone was naturally more yellow once both stones were set into the brooch. My friend was astonished, but the best part was yet to come. He purchased the more yellow diamond and was able to save $7,500 by doing so.

The overwhelming majority of diamonds used in commercial jewelry are so-called "white" diamonds. The rarest and most expensive "white" diamonds are totally colorless. Most diamonds display some degree of yellow or brown tint in their body color. The amount of yellow or brown tint that can be seen in a white diamond determines the color quality of the stone.

For years the general public has been told that the whiter or more colorless diamonds are the most beautiful. Consequently they have become the most sought after. Actually, this is totally untrue. What is true is that the more colorless diamonds occur far less frequently in nature. Therefore, the basis of diamond color grading, and the respective price per carat, is determined by rarity, not beauty. In my opinion, from the tens of thousands of diamonds I have viewed, if all other factors are equal, the diamonds that have some tint of yellow are more lively than their icy-looking, colorless, far more expensive counterparts.

The diamond grading system for "white" diamonds which is used most extensively by the diamond industry in the United States and Canada was developed by the Gemological Institute of America (GIA). This grading system awards the letter "D" to the most colorless grade of diamond and the letter "Z" to the diamonds with the most tint of yellow body color. The letters in descending order possess ever stronger tints of body color.

It is impossible to accurately evaluate the color of a diamond when it is mounted in a piece of jewelry. The tinge from the metal surrounding the diamond will reflect into the stone, preventing an accurate determination of the diamond's true color grade. In fact, the color grade of a diamond can be as much as four or five letters off in either direction, depending on the stone and the color of the precious metal. Very often this can work in your favor if you are buying a diamond to be set in yellow gold

COLORLESS	D
	E
	F
NEAR COLORLESS	G
	H
	I
	J
FAINT YELLOWISH TINT	K
	L
	M
VERY LIGHT YELLOWISH TINT	N
	O
	P
	Q
	R
TINTED LIGHT YELLOWISH	S
	T
	U
	V
	W
	X
	Y
	Z

Diamond Color Grading Chart

jewelry. In this case a yellowish diamond can appear quite a bit whiter than it actually is. Naturally a more yellowish stone will cost considerably less than its whiter counterpart. If you so desire, you will be able to purchase a larger "yellowish" diamond for the same amount of money you might have spent on a smaller, whiter stone. Ironically, a whiter stone when placed in a yellow setting can look considerably darker, thereby nullifying one of the most important reasons for purchasing a whiter stone. To the untrained eye, the whiter diamond and the yellow diamond will probably look very similar, if not the same.

Another characteristic that may affect a diamond's body color is the stone's fluorescence. This is a trait that some stones exhibit, causing them to appear to be different colors in different lights. A diamond that fluoresces might look whiter than it actually is in certain light. This is one reason why the color of any diamond over a half carat should always be authenticated by a Diamond Grading Report issued by the Gemological Institute of America's (GIA) Gem Trade Laboratory, Inc. To be certain that the true body color is being graded, the GIA will test for fluorescence with a special piece of equipment called an ultraviolet lamp prior to color grading.

If a diamond fluoresces, it usually will exhibit a bluish, yellowish, or whitish glow when examined in direct sunlight or daylight-type fluorescent lighting. Blue fluorescence occurs more frequently than yellow or white. Some white diamonds that exhibit a blue fluorescence may appear "blue-white" in the proper light. Ordinarily, you will not actually see any tint of fluorescence with the naked eye.

To prevent any disagreeable surprises it is important to know whether your diamond fluoresces prior to purchase. If, for example, you purchase a diamond that appeared to have a white body color in the jeweler's store under fluorescent lighting and it maintains its white body color in daylight but turns unexplainably yellow at night, you have more than likely purchased a fluorescent stone. The thing to keep in mind is, whatever color the fluorescence exhibits, it will only occur under fluorescent lighting or in the daylight. Incandescent or evening light will reveal the diamond's true body color.

CHAPTER 6

Clarity Grading

Due to my economic circumstances I did not buy my wife an engagement ring prior to our marriage. This was a source of great embarrassment for both of us, and a few years later, when my financial situation improved, I decided to purchase a diamond for my wife. Since I was living in Montreal at the time, I went to New York City to purchase a stone from a prominent diamond importer with whom I was doing business.

I looked at a number of diamonds before deciding on a particular stone. The diamond I picked was a well-proportioned, 2.28-carat, round, brilliant-cut stone with a tinge of yellowish body color that had the clarity grade of *slightly imperfect 2*. This diamond had a number of different internal flaws, the worst of which was a crystal in the very center of the table that reflected black.

The diamond merchant I was dealing with was surprised by my choice. He pointed out that he had a number of small diamonds to choose from, in the same price range, that were better quality in that they were either whiter in body color or had fewer internal imperfections. Carefully he put three other stones next to the diamond I had selected. We discussed the merits of each stone.

Finally, I asked his receptionist, a twenty-two-year-old single woman who knew nothing about the quality of diamonds, which stone she liked. After looking at all four stones for a few moments she picked the diamond that I had selected. Her boss asked her why she selected that particular stone. "Because it's the biggest," she replied.

I ended up buying the diamond and my wife, who is a diamond expert, is happily wearing it to this day. The point of this anecdote is that the clarity and color grade assigned to a specific diamond have far more to do with the rarity of the stone than its beauty. A great many of the inclusions that a diamond may have are so small that they can only be seen by using a ten-power loupe. These tiny imperfections normally have no effect on the reflective quality of a diamond. The only imperfections that may affect the radiance of a stone are those that may be seen without the aid of a loupe, and even that is questionable. Therefore, it is possible to purchase a larger or whiter stone by sacrificing on the degree of clarity. What is important is that you know with certainty the clarity grade of the diamond you are considering purchasing.

The following chart illustrates the diamond grading system that is the industry standard in North America. It was developed by the Gemological Institute of America and is used on their Diamond Grading Reports. Rapaport, the New York company that monitors the wholesale price of diamonds, also uses this clarity grading system in their reports.

GIA CLARITY GRADES

FL	Flawless
IF	Internally Flawless
VVS1	Very, Very Slightly Imperfect 1 and 2
VVS2	
VS1	Very Slightly Imperfect 1 and 2
VS2	
SI1	Slightly Imperfect 1 and 2
SI2	
I1	Imperfect 1, 2, and 3
I2	
I3	

Clarity Grade	Number and Size of Imperfections	Visible with the Loupe	Visible without the Loupe	Effect on Brilliancy
IF	No imperfections	Nothing to see	Not visible	None
VVS_1	A few very, very small imperfections	Very difficult to see	Not visible	Not diminished
VVS_2	A few more very, very small imperfections	Difficult to see	Not visible	Not diminished
VS_1	Some very small imperfections	Can be seen	Not visible	Not diminished
VS_2	Some more very small imperfections	Easier to see	Not visible	Not diminished
SI_1	A number of small imperfections	Easily seen	Not visible	Not diminished
SI_2	A greater number of small imperfections	Very easily seen	Very hard to see	Not diminished
I_1	Large imperfections	Immediately visible	Hard to see	Not diminished
I_2	Many fairly large imperfections	Immediately visible	Can be seen	Slightly diminished
I_3	Many very large imperfections	Immediately visible	Easily seen	Considerably diminished

Clarity-Grading Chart

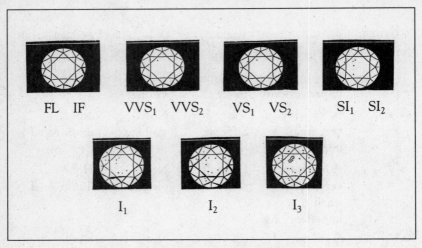

Clarity-Grading Examples

The definition of these terms are:

1. FLAWLESS (FL)

These stones have no internal flaws or external blemishes when viewed by an expert through a ten-power loupe. These stones are extremely rare, and are hardly ever used in jewelry. They are investment-grade diamonds, sell at very high prices, and normally are stored in bank vaults. Wearing stones of this quality could cause them to be damaged by chipping the stone or breaking the culet, thereby losing their flawless status.

2. INTERNALLY FLAWLESS (IF)

These diamonds have no internal flaws when viewed by an expert diamond grader under a ten-power loupe, but they do have minor external blemishes that can be removed by repolishing the surface of the stone. These stones are extremely rare, and are hardly ever used in jewelry. They are investment-grade diamonds, sell at very high prices, and normally are stored in bank vaults. Wearing stones of this quality could cause them to be damaged by chipping the stone or breaking the culet, thereby losing their flawless status.

3. VERY, VERY SLIGHTLY IMPERFECT (VVS)

This category of diamonds comes in two grades (1 and 2). They are stones in which the internal imperfections are very, very difficult to see by an expert under ten-power magnification. These stones are also very rare and consequently very expensive. In sizes of a half carat and greater, they are not often used in commercial jewelry.

4. VERY SLIGHTLY IMPERFECT (VS)

This category of diamonds comes in two grades (1 and 2). They are stones that have internal flaws that are difficult for an expert diamond grader to see with the aid of a ten-power magnification.

5. SLIGHTLY IMPERFECT (SI)

This category of diamonds comes in two grades (1 and 2). They have flaws that are easy for an expert diamond grader to see with the aid of ten-power magnification, and in some instances the flaws may be seen without the aid of magnification. Diamonds in this category are not very rare, are lower in price than the above categories, and their optical beauty is not disturbed by the various small internal imperfections. I highly recommend this category of diamonds for purchase and use in commercial jewelry. Furthermore, these diamonds are normally the easiest to resell or replace due to their popularity and practicability.

6. IMPERFECT (I)

This classification of diamonds comes in three grades (1, 2, and 3). They normally have flaws that are easily visible to an expert diamond grader without the use of magnification. The I3 grade diamonds are normally of extremely poor quality and exhibit very little brilliance and fire. Under most circumstances I would recommend that consumers not buy diamonds with I2 or I3 clarity classifications. There is very little beauty to these stones, and their flaws may be serious enough to result in tension within the stone, which may cause them to break or shatter during the course of normal wear. I do recommend that you seriously consider an I1 grade of diamond when you are in the market to purchase a stone of one-half carat size or greater. The dollar saving on diamonds purchased at this quality level should be significant without a substantial loss of optical beauty.

The key to clarity classification is to know precisely what the actual grade of the stone is and how the diamond visually appeals to you. The means of determining the precise grading information will be covered in Chapter 8.

CLARITY ENHANCEMENT

Thanks to modern technological advances, today it is possible to improve the clarity of a diamond. The two most often used techniques for clarity enhancement are fracture filling and lasering.

Fracture filling

A large imperfection(s) that can be seen without the aid of magnification may be concealed in lower-grade diamonds (SI and I) by filling them with a colorless, glasslike substance. The results of fracture filling may not be permanent; inappropriate handling can cause the filler to leave the stone or change color.

I strongly recommend that you do not purchase a fracture-filled stone because some faults are serious enough to create structural weakness within the stone, making splitting or chipping of the diamond more likely during normal wear. Even though the prices of fracture-filled diamonds are considerably lower, this is a risky way to save money because you will not know how badly or seriously the diamond was flawed prior to being filled.

There is only one sure way that you can protect yourself from buying a fracture-filled diamond without knowing it. The GIA will not issue a diamond grading report on a filled diamond. As long as you purchase a diamond accompanied by a genuine, corresponding GIA Diamond Grading Report you will never be tricked into buying a fracture-filled diamond.

If you decide to purchase a fracture-filled diamond, make certain that you are paying at least 30 percent below the correct color grade and I3 clarity grade designation on the Rapaport Diamond Report (Chapter 9). The only reason you, as a

Diamond with Laser Drill Holes. Photograph courtesy of © GIA
(Gemological Institute of America)

consumer, would even consider this type of diamond is because you can buy it inexpensively.

Lasering

By employing laser technology it is possible to make flaws in diamonds less visible. As I have previously explained I personally do not believe that this process adds any significant beauty to the stone. Lasering does not normally damage the structural integrity of the diamond and does not affect the durability of the stone. The effects of the laser treatment are permanent and irreversible. Lastly, the GIA will issue a Diamond Grading Report on a lasered diamond, stating that the diamond has been lasered. Therefore, you will always know if the stone you are purchasing is a lasered diamond if you follow my advice and only buy stones accompanied by a GIA Diamond Grading Report.

Lasering makes a stone less expensive to purchase. Refer to the proper classifications on the Rapaport Diamond Report (Chapter 9) and deduct at least 30 percent for a lasered stone. For example, if a J color, SI2 1.00-carat round, brilliant-cut diamond sold for $3,000 per carat, the same stone, if it had been lasered, would sell for $2,100 per carat or less.

CHAPTER 7

Cut or Make

EVALUATING THE PROPORTIONS OF THE DIAMOND

Imagine what an elegant gown using the finest fabrics available would look like if the pattern were incorrectly cut. Obviously the dress would never look good.

It works exactly the same way with diamonds. Regardless of how good the color and clarity grades are, a badly proportioned diamond will look dull, lifeless, or larger or smaller than its actual weight. Some cutting defects such as a very thin girdle can weaken the stone and make it more vulnerable to breaking or chipping. Most diamond merchants consider the proportions and finish of the stone the most important consideration when they purchase a stone. The terms "cut" or "make" refer to how well the stone is manufactured.

A rough diamond is not beautiful. In fact, it looks like a broken piece of frosted glass. It is up to the diamond cutter to fashion the stone so its potential beauty is released. There are a number of factors in the cutting and polishing of the stone that determine whether or not a diamond achieves its potential beauty.

Diamonds, due to factors such as the shape of the rough material and the economics of weight retention, are cut into many different shapes. **When asked, I strongly recommend purchasing a round, brilliant-cut diamond over any other shape.** The reason is that when a stone is well proportioned, its shape displays the

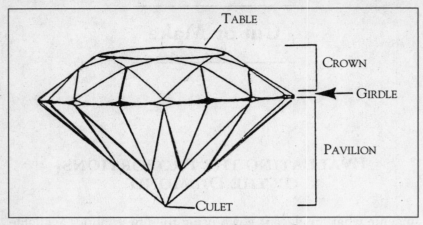

Parts of a Faceted Diamond

greatest amount of brilliance and fire. This particular style of cut combined with the optical properties of diamonds allows most of the light passing into the stone to be reflected back through the top of the gem. Therefore the round, brilliant-cut diamond will have greater scintillation and liveliness, overall, than any other shape into which diamonds are fashioned.

The above diagram illustrates a round, brilliant-cut diamond. The top is called the crown. The crown is composed of crown facets and a table. The diameter of the stone is called the girdle. The bottom part of the diamond is the pavilion. The culet is the point facet on the bottom of the pavilion.

Over the years I have developed a personal step-by-step procedure for judging the proportions or cutting quality of a round, brilliant-cut diamond. It has worked well for me and I would like to share it with you.

1. The first thing I do is visually inspect the diamond. If the stone displays a great deal of brilliance and fire, then the cutting and proportioning are probably acceptable. If the stone seems dark, lifeless, or dead in the center, or if the girdle appears thick,

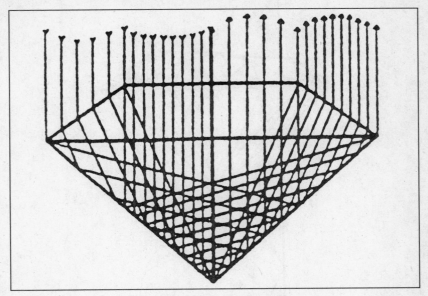

Light Ideally Reflected

the cut or make of the stone is poor. In addition, I look for obvious cutting faults such as an out-of-round diamond or a broken culet.

2. My next step is to determine whether the diamond is "round" or "out-of-round." Using a very accurate millimeter gauge I carefully measure the diameter of the diamond at a number of different points along the girdle. What I am looking for are the highest and lowest measurements of the diameter of the stone. The difference between the highest and lowest measurements will determine whether or not a diamond is round. For example, the ideal diameter of a one-carat diamond should measure 6.50 millimeters. If the ideal stone is truly round it would measure 6.50 millimeters at every point on the diameter. Recognizing that truly round diamonds are extremely rare, some variation is allowed, and the stone will not be considered "out-of-round" unless it varies by more than the established

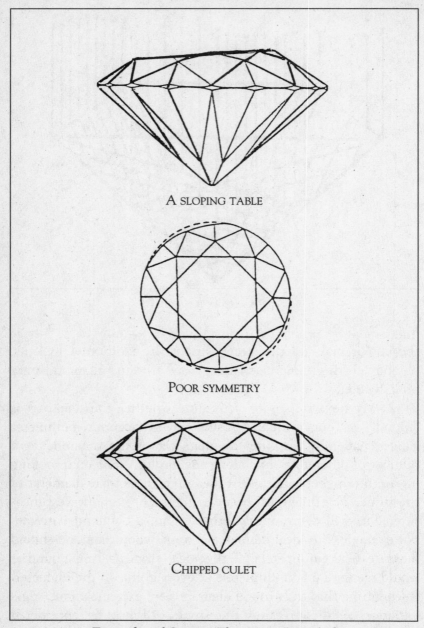

A SLOPING TABLE

POOR SYMMETRY

CHIPPED CULET

Examples of Cutting Flaws in a Diamond

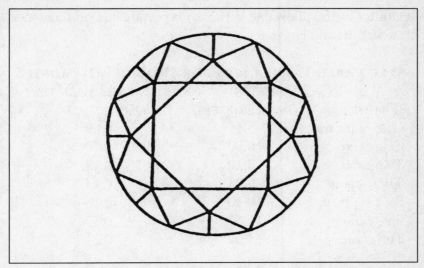

Cutting Flaws in a Diamond (Out-of-Round Girdle)

standard—approximately 0.10 millimeter (one-tenth of a millimeter) in a one-carat stone.

To determine whether a diamond is round, simply subtract the smallest millimeter measurement from the highest measurement. In a one-carat stone, if the deviation is 0.10 millimeter or less, the stone is considered "round." If the discrepancy is greater than 0.10 millimeter, the diamond is "out-of-round." For example, if a one-carat diamond has a high measurement of 6.61 millimeters and a low measurement of 6.50 millimeters, then the stone is "out-of-round" because it exceeds the established standard of 0.10 millimeter (6.61 mm − 6.50 mm = 0.11 mm). On the other hand, if the high measurement of a one-carat diamond is 6.59 mm and the low measurement is 6.50 mm, then the stone is "round" because it does not exceed the established standard of 0.10 millimeter (6.59 mm − 6.50 mm = 0.09 mm). The following chart lists the established standard variations in millimeters for a number of different size round diamonds. Some flexibility in the allowable variation is permissible on diamonds of two carats and larger.

ALLOWABLE TOLERANCES FOR "ROUND" DIAMONDS

WEIGHT	DIAMETER (IN MILLIMETERS)	ALLOWABLE VARIATION (IN MILLIMETERS)
One-half carat	5.15	0.09
One carat	6.50	0.10
Two carat	8.20	0.12
Three carat	9.35	0.14
Four carat	10.30	0.16
Five carat	11.10	0.17
Ten carat	14.00	0.21

3. My next test is to determine the depth percentage of the

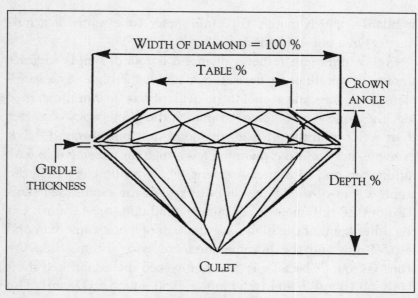

Depth Percentage

round diamond I am evaluating. The depth percentage is the distance from the table to the culet as a percentage of the average diameter measurement of the stone. For example, the depth of a stone is 4.11 mm, the high diameter measurement is 7.18 mm, and the low measurement is 7.11 mm. To obtain the depth percentage we first average the high and low diameter measurements. This yields an average diameter of 7.14 mm (7.11 + 7.18 = 14.29 divided by 2 = 7.14). We then divide 4.11 mm (the depth) by the 7.14 mm (average diameter) to obtain the depth percentage, which in this case is 57.5 percent.

Another example is a diamond with a low diameter measurement of 8.09 mm and a high diameter measurement of 8.19 mm. The depth of the stone is 4.97 mm. The first step is to derive the average diameter by adding the two measurements together and dividing by 2 (8.09 mm + 8.19 mm = 16.28 divided by 2 = 8.14 mm). We then divide 4.97 mm (the depth) by the 8.14 mm (average diameter) to obtain the depth percentage, which in this case is 61.0 percent.

A round, brilliant-cut diamond with a depth percentage between 58 and 64 percent is usually a pleasing stone. Stones with depth percentages above 67 percent and below 55 percent *should not be purchased*. If the depth percentage is too high (above 67 percent) the stone will look smaller than its carat weight indicates and will be too deep to display maximum brilliance and fire. If the depth percentage is extremely high, brilliance will be severely reduced and the center can look dark and lifeless. If the depth percentage is too low (below 55 percent) brilliance will be significantly reduced.

The following three diagrams illustrate the results of different types of depth percentages on the liveliness of a round, brilliant-cut diamond. In the first, the bottom of the stone, known as the pavilion, is too heavy and the light is not entirely reflected back to the top of the stone. This generally is the result

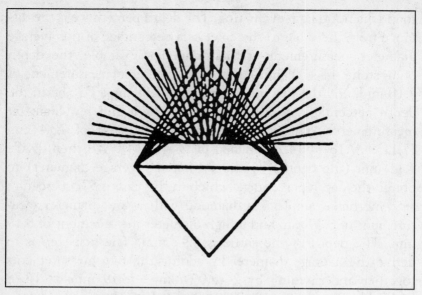

Pavilion Proportions (Too Heavy)

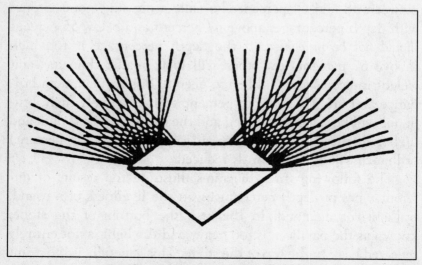

Pavilion Proportions (Too Shallow)

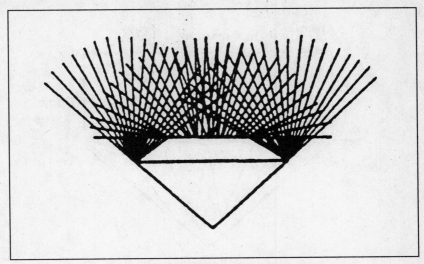

Pavilion Proportions (Cut Perfectly)

of the depth percentage being greater than 65 percent. In the second, the pavilion is too shallow, resulting in light not being reflected from the top, which is known as the table. This is the result of the depth percentage being below 57 percent. In the last, the diamond is perfectly proportioned and the total brilliance and fire are dispersed throughout the crown.

4. Another significant test is the table percentage. The table percentage is derived by dividing the diameter of the table by the diameter of the entire stone. For example, the first stone we evaluated had an average total diameter of 7.14 mm. The diameter of the table of this stone is 4.57 mm. Therefore, the table percentage is 64 percent (4.57 mm divided by 7.14 mm).

In our second example the average total diameter of the stone is 8.14 mm. The table diameter measures 5.29 mm. Therefore, the table percentage is 65 percent (5.29 mm divided by 8.14 mm). Round, brilliant-cut diamonds made with tables ranging from 53 percent to 64 percent are normally pleasing,

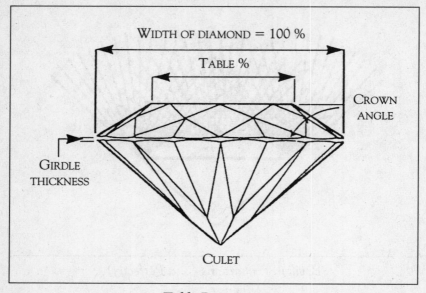

Table Percentage

lively stones. Diamonds with smaller tables normally display more fire than those with larger tables. Diamonds with larger tables have less fire but can have greater brilliance. Table width affects the diamond's character, but deciding which character is

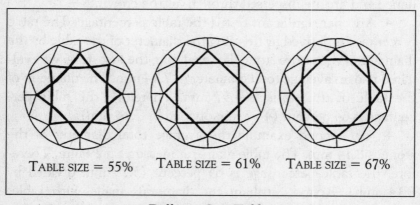

Different Size Tables

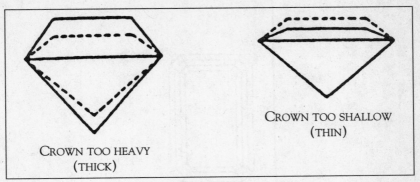

CROWN TOO SHALLOW
(THIN)

CROWN TOO HEAVY
(THICK)

Proportions

more pleasing is a matter of individual preference. I would avoid purchasing stones with a table percentage above 68 percent or below 52 percent. The tables will either be too large or too small and they will not display the maximum amount of beauty or liveliness.

FANCY-SHAPE DIAMONDS

All diamonds that are not round are considered fancy shapes. Their shapes include marquise, pear, oval, heart-shaped, emerald-cut, tapered baguette, baguette, radiant and trilliant, among other styles both old and new. Fancy shapes, unlike the round, brilliant-cut diamond, do not have a precise cutting formula. Their proportioning is most often determined by the shape and quality of the rough material. This makes the evaluation of the cut or make of the finished fancy stone far more arbitrary. Each stone needs to be visually inspected to determine its brilliance and fire, as well as what cutting faults exist.

The most common fault in fancy stones, particularly marquise and pear shapes, is the bow tie, or butterfly effect. Practically all modern cut fancy shapes will exhibit some bow tie

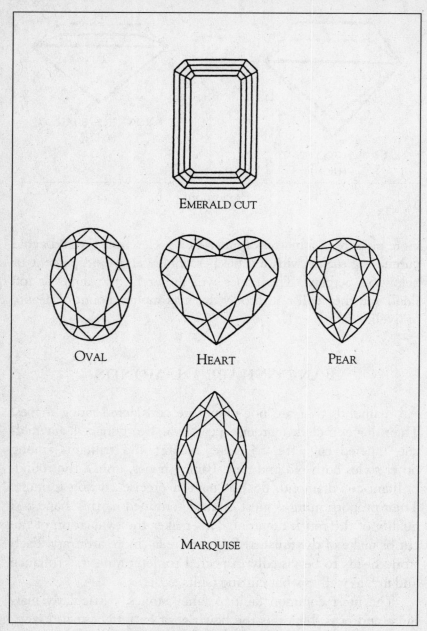

EMERALD CUT

OVAL   HEART   PEAR

MARQUISE

Fancy Cut Diamonds

MARQUISE WITH A LARGE BOW TIE

Flaws in Cut—Fancy-Shape Diamonds

effect. Depending on the cut, this is a darkened area across the center or widest part of the stone. The larger, more pronounced the bow tie, the poorer the proportioning of the stone.

Fancy-shape diamonds can have many of the same cutting

Large Bow Tie in Marquise Diamond. Photograph courtesy of © GIA (Gemological Institute of America)

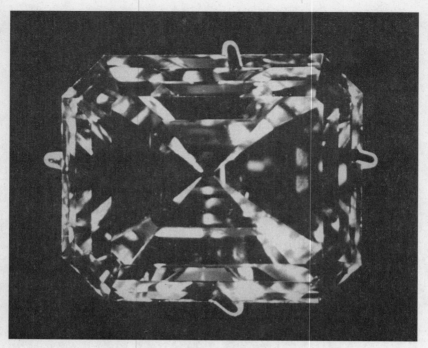

*Deep Emerald-Cut Diamond with a Black Cross. Photograph
courtesy of © GIA (Gemological Institute of America)*

faults as round, brilliant-cut diamonds. They may be cut too
broad or too narrow, non-symmetrically, their tables too large or
too small, and their crowns or pavilions can be too deep or too
shallow. A problem unique to some styles of fancy shapes, such
as marquise and pear shapes, is that they have pointed ends or
corners that are susceptible to breakage if their girdles are very
thin or the stone is subjected to a forceful blow.

Personal preferences will always play a role in the selection
of fancy shapes; some prefer a narrow, longer marquise, for
example, while others prefer a shorter, fatter one. Whatever
the shape you are considering, you must ask yourself whether
or not you find the stone pleasing. Does it have an exciting

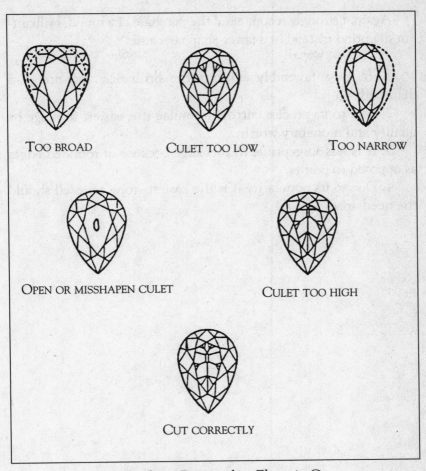

TOO BROAD   CULET TOO LOW   TOO NARROW

OPEN OR MISSHAPEN CULET   CULET TOO HIGH

CUT CORRECTLY

Fancy-Shape Diamonds—Flaws in Cut

personality? Does it exhibit a great deal of brilliance and fire? Is the diamond uniformly brilliant, or does it have dead spots? Are there any cutting faults, such as a very thin girdle, that make it more susceptible to breakage? After viewing a number of fancy-shape diamonds and considering all these factors, you must ultimately make the decision based on your personal taste.

Again, I strongly recommend the purchase of a round, brilliant-cut diamond instead of a fancy shape because:

1. It most favorably exhibits the brilliance and fire of a diamond;

2. Due to its precise cutting formulae it is easiest to judge its quality and monetary worth;

3. It is less susceptible to breakage because of rounded edges as opposed to points;

4. Due to its popularity it is the easiest stone to resell should the need arise.

CHAPTER 8

The GIA Diamond Grading Report

Would you accept delivery of a new car without receiving an official registration certificate from the Motor Vehicles Bureau? The registration clearly states the make and model of the vehicle, the year it was manufactured, the vehicle's identification number, and a description of other characteristics that clearly demonstrate that the vehicle you are driving belongs to you.

Would you purchase a home without transferring the title and receiving a deed to that property? The deed will specify the official government folio number of the property, the location and size of the land lot, and the improvements on the land which should include any structures such as a house. The description of the house will include the liveable square footage, number of bedrooms, bathrooms, etc. Without a valid deed you would have a difficult time proving ownership of the property.

Why would you consider buying a diamond without receiving some sort of independent, third-party, unbiased documentation confirming that you are in fact buying a diamond and what the quality and characteristics of that diamond are? You are not a diamond expert! You cannot rely on the word or certificate of the one who wants to sell you the stone as an honest, disinterested opinion because the seller has a vested interest, namely to make a profit. When you are ready to purchase a diamond you need to trust a reliable, impartial laboratory for a factual diamond grading report.

When purchasing a diamond a half-carat in weight (.50 ct.) or larger I would not buy a stone unless it came with a Diamond

Grading Report from the Gemological Institute of America. The GIA is a world-renowned, non-profit, professional institution that promotes education in the jewelry industry. They have established the GIA Gem Trade Laboratory (GIA Gem Trade Laboratory is a division of GIA Enterprises, Inc., a wholly owned subsidiary of the non-profit Gemological Institute of America) with locations in New York City and Carlsbad, California (see Appendix C for addresses). This laboratory issues Diamond Grading Reports that describe and analyze the quality and physical characteristics of diamonds. There are a number of other organizations that issue Diamond Grading Reports, but I would only accept a report issued by the GIA because their reports are recognized worldwide. Due to their accuracy and neutrality these reports are the ultimate word on the quality of a stone. There are no arguments, no disputes, no protests. Their word is final and in the jewelry industry their word is law!

The GIA Diamond Grading Report is also indispensable for insurance appraisals. Even though the report never estimates the monetary value of the diamond, the description of the stone is so complete that there is virtually no way that a dispute can arise as to the weight, shape, or quality of the stone. Therefore, the insurer is bound, by the facts of the report, to replace precisely the same size, shape, and quality diamond. If, for whatever reason, there is a legal dispute, the GIA Diamond Grading Report is held in such high esteem that it may be used as evidence in a court of law.

The GIA Diamond Grading Report is very useful in determining the identity of a diamond. Let's suppose that you are going shopping for a diamond. You go to a diamond merchant and see a stone you like. The merchant quotes a price for the diamond and you ask for a photocopy of the GIA Diamond Grading Report. A week later you return to this merchant to purchase the diamond. How can you be certain that he has not sold the stone you wanted to buy and now is showing you another one? By having a copy of the GIA Diamond Grading Report it is possible for you to have an independent expert evaluate the stone to determine that the diamond and the report correspond.

The Rapaport Diamond Corporation monitors the wholesale cash asking prices of diamonds in New York City. They publish a price list based on diamonds that have GIA Diamond Grading Reports, also known in the jewelry trade as a GIA certification. Therefore, the GIA Diamond Grading Report helps establish the wholesale prices for different sizes, shapes, and qualities of diamonds. By knowing how to read and interpret the GIA report and by using the Rapaport Diamond Report you can determine the New York wholesale cash asking price of almost any diamond. This is essential information when buying or selling a diamond.

How to Read
a GIA Diamond Grading Report

The following illustration is a sample of an actual GIA Diamond Grading Report.

The following opinions on how to read and interpret the GIA Diamond Grading Report are strictly those of the author based upon his formal education and his twenty-five years of practical experience in the jewelry industry. They do not represent the opinions of the Gemological Institute of America, any of their subsidiary companies, or any of their employees.

The reason for this disclaimer is that the GIA does not grade the quality of the cut or make of diamonds. They only measure a diamond and describe the ratio of the major physical features of a diamond such as depth percentage and table percentage. Since I am of the very strong opinion that cut is by far the most important element in the overall quality of a diamond, I have

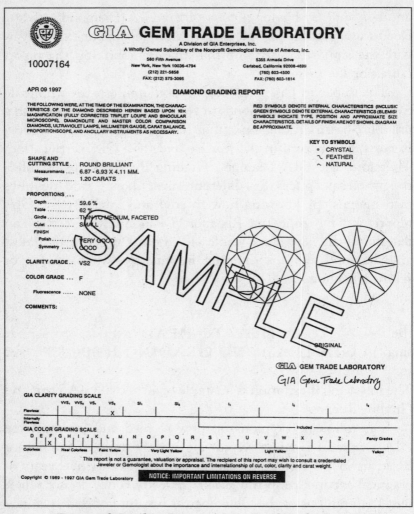

GIA GEM TRADE LABORATORY

A Division of GIA Enterprises, Inc.
A Wholly Owned Subsidiary of the Nonprofit Gemological Institute of America, Inc.

10007164

580 Fifth Avenue
New York, New York 10036-4794
(212) 221-5858
FAX: (212) 575-3095

5355 Armada Drive
Carlsbad, California 92008-4699
(760) 603-4500
FAX: (760) 603-1814

APR 09 1997   **DIAMOND GRADING REPORT**

THE FOLLOWING WERE, AT THE TIME OF THE EXAMINATION, THE CHARAC-
TERISTICS OF THE DIAMOND DESCRIBED HEREIN BASED UPON 10X
MAGNIFICATION (FULLY CORRECTED TRIPLET LOUPE AND BINOCULAR
MICROSCOPE), DIAMONDLITE AND MASTER COLOR COMPARISON
DIAMONDS, ULTRAVIOLET LAMPS, MILLIMETER GAUGE, CARAT BALANCE,
PROPORTIONSCOPE, AND ANCILLARY INSTRUMENTS AS NECESSARY.

RED SYMBOLS DENOTE INTERNAL CHARACTERISTICS (INCLUSIC
GREEN SYMBOLS DENOTE EXTERNAL CHARACTERISTICS (BLEMIS)
SYMBOLS INDICATE TYPE, POSITION AND APPROXIMATE SIZE
CHARACTERISTICS. DETAILS OF FINISH ARE NOT SHOWN. DIAGRAM
BE APPROXIMATE.

KEY TO SYMBOLS
∘ CRYSTAL
⌐ FEATHER
∼ NATURAL

SHAPE AND
CUTTING STYLE .. ROUND BRILLIANT
 Measurements .... 6.87 - 6.93 X 4.11 MM.
 Weight .... 1.20 CARATS

PROPORTIONS ...
 Depth .... 59.6 %
 Table .... 62 %
 Girdle .... THIN TO MEDIUM, FACETED
 Culet .... SMALL
 FINISH
  Polish .... VERY GOOD
  Symmetry ...... GOOD

CLARITY GRADE .. VS2

COLOR GRADE ... F

Fluorescence ...... NONE

COMMENTS:

ORIGINAL

GIA GEM TRADE LABORATORY
GIA Gem Trade Laboratory

GIA CLARITY GRADING SCALE

	FL	IF	VVS₁	VVS₂	VS₁	VS₂	SI₁	SI₂	I₁	I₂	I₃
Flawless						X					

Internally
Flawless

Included

GIA COLOR GRADING SCALE

D	E	F	G	H	I	J	K	L	M	N	O	P	Q	R	S	T	U	V	W	X	Y	Z	Fancy Grades
	X																						

Colorless | Near Colorless | Faint Yellow | Very Light Yellow | Light Yellow | Yellow

This report is not a guarantee, valuation or appraisal. The recipient of this report may wish to consult a credentialed
Jeweler or Gemologist about the importance and interrelationship of cut, color, clarity and carat weight.

Copyright © 1989 - 1997 GIA Gem Trade Laboratory   **NOTICE: IMPORTANT LIMITATIONS ON REVERSE**

Diamond Grading Report (Gem Trade Laboratory)

interpreted this raw data and expressed my views as to what con-
stitutes a well-cut stone as opposed to a poorly proportioned one.
This information is absolutely essential if you are going to purchase a diamond intelligently.

1. **Date** consists of the month, day, and year the report was issued. If the date is not recent it is important to check the diamond to be certain that it has not been damaged or re-cut since the report was issued. In our sample report the date is April 9, 1997.

2. **Gem Identification** is verified by the title of the report. The GIA only issues Diamond Grading Reports to gems identi-fied as genuine diamonds.

3. **Report Identification Number** is the unique number assigned to this report from GIA for reference purposes. If a duplicate report is required, this number must be given to GIA so they may find the needed information. In our sample the report identification number is 10007164.

4. **Shape and Cutting Style** specifies the form and cutting style of the diamond. In the example the diamond's shape is round and the cutting style is brilliant.

5. **Measurement** has to do with the physical dimensions of the diamond. In round diamonds the first two numbers are the smallest and largest diameters of the diamond measured to the hundredth of a millimeter. In our example the smallest diameter is 6.87 millimeters and widest is 6.93 millimeters. The third number represents the actual depth of the stone. The depth is measured from the top of the table to the end of the culet. In our example the depth of the diamond is 4.11 millimeters. Please note that in fancy-shape diamonds the first two numbers indi-cate the length (top to bottom) and width (left to right) of the diamond (see Special Considerations Used for Fancy-Shape Dia-monds at the end of this chapter). The third number is the depth of the stone, which is measured from the table to the culet.

6. **Weight** is an accurate determination of the heaviness in carat(s) and/or points of the diamond described in the report (see Chapter 4). In our example the diamond weighs 1.20 carats or 120 points.

The combination of measurements, description, and weight

is extremely useful in determining whether the diamond being inspected is the same diamond as the one described on the grading report. If the measurements and/or weight are not the same the diamond must be carefully scrutinized.

7. **Proportions** is the section of the GIA Diamond Grading Report that examines how well the diamond is cut, whether the proportions or "make" of the stone allow the maximum brilliance and fire to be released. The information concerning the proportions is extremely important in evaluating round, brilliant-cut diamonds; however, it is of little use when evaluating the cut or make of fancy-shape diamonds. With fancy-shape stones it is necessary to visually determine whether or not the stone is too

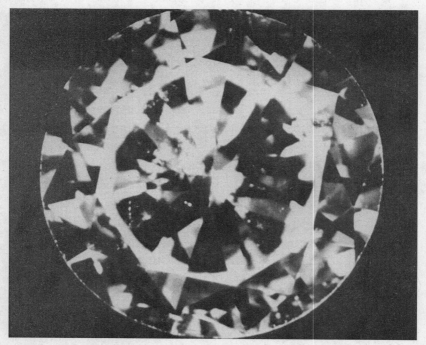

Fish-Eye Diamond with a Shallow Pavilion. Photograph courtesy of © GIA (Gemological Institute of America)

narrow, too wide, too deep, or too shallow. This lack of uniformity with fancy shapes makes the judgment of good proportioning more difficult and subjective.

8. **Depth** is a percentage calculated by measuring the depth of the stone (from the table to the culet) and dividing that number by the average width of the stone. In our sample report the depth percentage is 59.6 percent. This percentage was computed by dividing the actual depth of 4.11 mm by the average width of the stone, 6.90 mm (6.87 + 6.93 divided by 2 = 6.90 mm). The physical dimensions of the diamond were supplied earlier in the report under the measurements category. The depth percentage is one indicator of how well the diamond has been proportioned. **Stones having extremely thick or extremely thin girdles that have a depth percentage of 65 percent and above or 57 percent and below are normally poorly cut and should not be purchased!** The following chart summarizes the significance of the depth percentage if the girdle of the diamond is either extremely thick or extremely thin:

DEPTH PERCENTAGE

57 percent or less	Inferior
58 to 60 percent	Ideal
60 to 62 percent	Superior
62 to 64 percent	Good
64 to 65 percent	Fair
Above 65 percent	Inferior

9. **Table** is a percentage calculated by dividing the width of the table by the width of the entire stone. In our sample report the table percentage is 62 percent. Round diamonds with table percentages between 53 percent and 64 percent normally are attractive, lively stones. **Diamonds having extremely thick or extremely thin girdles with table percentages over 67 percent and below 53 percent are normally poorly cut and these stones**

should be not be purchased! The following chart summarizes the significance of the table percentage if the girdle of the diamond is either extremely thick or extremely thin:

TABLE PERCENTAGE

Below 53 percent	Inferior
53 to 58 percent	Ideal
58.1 to 60 percent	Superior
60.1 to 64 percent	Good
64.1 to 67 percent	Fair
67.1 percent and over	Inferior

10. The **Girdle** of a diamond is the circumference of the diamond where the top section of the stone (crown) meets the bottom section (pavilion). Even though diamonds are the hardest material known to man, they are brittle. If the outer edge

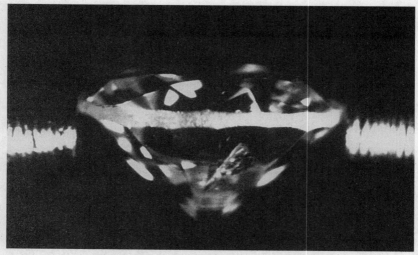

Thick Girdle. Photograph courtesy of © GIA
(Gemological Institute of America)

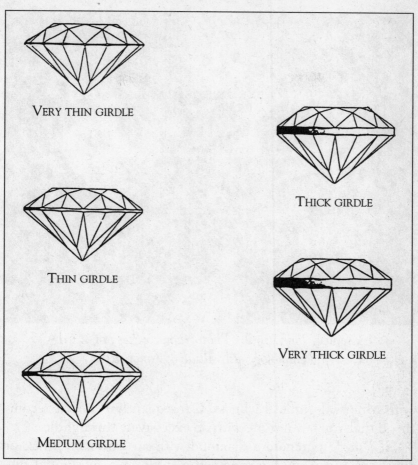

Girdle Thickness

of a stone is very thin it might be chipped during the course of normal wear. Therefore, I would recommend that you not purchase a diamond that has an extremely thin girdle.

A diamond with an extremely thick girdle is not desirable. It will look smaller than it should because extra weight is in the center of the stone. It will make the depth percentage larger than it should be and the diamond will not be as lively as a stone

*Extremely Thin Girdle. Photograph courtesy of © GIA
(Gemological Institute of America)*

with a normal girdle thickness. Consequently I do not recommend that you buy a stone with an excessively thick girdle.

If you do purchase a diamond with an extremely thick or thin girdle, you must purchase the stone at a substantial discount. In the sample report the girdle is acceptable, being described as thin to medium. This particular girdle was faceted as opposed to being left unpolished, which is normally the case. The reason for polishing (faceting) a girdle is to remove an imperfection or a missing space.

11. The **Culet** is the small, flat facet on the pointed bottom of the pavilion, parallel to the table of the stone. Ideally the culet should be graded as very small or small. The reason is that the larger the culet the more visible it will be from the top

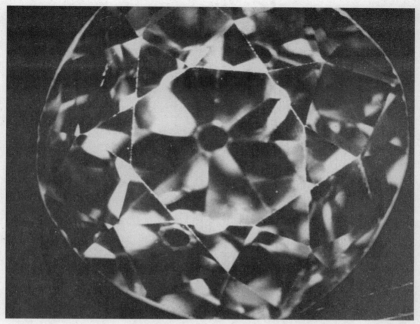

Very Large Culet. Photograph courtesy of © GIA
(Gemological Institute of America)

(table) of the stone, and that is not desirable. Diamonds that have large culets, broken culets, open culets, and very off-center culets should not be purchased unless very large discounts are offered and you do not mind how these defects affect the beauty of the stone. Some of these conditions, such as broken culets and open culets, can be repaired by recutting the stone, but you will incur additional expense and normally lose carat weight in the process. I do not recommend you get involved with recutting stones; that is something best left to the diamond professionals. In the sample used the culet is graded as small.

    12. The next category on the GIA Diamond Grading Report is the **Finish** of the diamond. The finish refers to the quality and care the diamond cutter took in making sure that the facets of

the crown and pavilion were properly aligned (symmetry) and that the final polishing of the stone was properly done.

If the symmetry of the diamond is not good the light entering the stone will not be properly reflected and the stone will not have as much fire or brilliance as it should have. If the symmetry grade is fair then there is something out of alignment and the stone must be purchased at a substantial discount. I would not purchase a diamond that has a symmetry grade of poor because the beauty of the stone will be very much diminished.

The polishing grade given to a diamond can be *excellent, very good, good, fair,* or *poor.* As the polishing grade goes down so does the price of the diamond. The good news is that the stone can be repolished and the grade can normally be improved to almost any level desired. If a dealer offers you a stone with a fair or poor

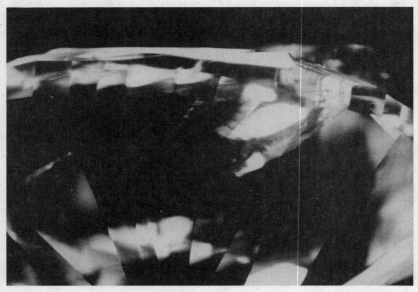

Imperfection in the Pavilion. Photograph courtesy of © GIA
(Gemological Institute of America)

polishing grade that you would like to buy, simply ask him to have the stone repolished and recertify the stone. You might have to add a little extra money to the price of the stone to cover these expenses, but it will be worth it. Normally repolishing the stone will not cause it to lose very much weight, and all the other categories on the report should remain the same. Our sample report graded the diamond's polish as very good and its symmetry as good.

13. The **Clarity Grade** of a diamond is shown on the report, as well as on the first bar index on the bottom of the page. In our sample report the diamond is graded as a VS2 stone (very slightly imperfect 2nd degree). For a full discussion of how clarity grades are determined refer to Chapter 6. Generally I like

Dark Imperfections in a Diamond. Photograph courtesy of © GIA
(Gemological Institute of America)

to look at the diamond before making a final judgment, but as a rule I would not advise you to purchase any diamond below the clarity grade of I1.

14. The **Color Grade** of a diamond is shown on the report and on the second bar index at the bottom of the page. In our sample report the diamond received the color grade of F. For a complete explanation of how color grade is determined refer to Chapter 5. Color grade is a personal preference, but because of dollar value and general appearance I prefer diamonds between the color grade of I and R for commercial jewelry.

15. Every diamond that the GIA analyzes is tested for **Fluorescence** (see Chapter 5). If present it will be graded by the GIA as *faint, medium, strong,* or *very strong.* The color of the fluorescence, such as yellow or blue, is indicated in grades of medium, strong, or very strong. If fluorescence is indicated on the report it is essential that the stone be examined in daylight or under fluorescent light. If the appearance of the stone is cloudy or oily this indicates that the stone has a very strong blue fluorescence and because of its diminished beauty and value I would not purchase this diamond. Additionally, if a diamond has a moderate to very strong yellow fluorescence it will appear more yellow in daylight and under fluorescent lighting. To determine the actual color the diamond must be examined at night or under incandescent lighting, when the stone will not fluoresce. A diamond with this characteristic, if purchased, must be purchased at a substantial discount.

16. **Comments** is the area where remarks concerning the diamond are written that are not illustrated on the plotting diagram. For example, if a stone has a crown angle, the angle at which the crown facets were cut, that indicates that the stone was poorly proportioned, and that statement might be indicated here. The fact that the diamond has been laser treated might be recorded here.

CROWN ANGLE TABLE

35 Degrees and Above	Poor
34 to 35 Degrees	Excellent
32 to 33.9 Degrees	Good
30 to 31.9 Degrees	Fair
29.9 or Less	Poor

17. The **Plotting Diagram** indicates the type and placement of the diamond's internal and external imperfections. This graphic data is another excellent tool that an expert may use to identify and evaluate the stone.

PROBLEMS WITH THE GIA DIAMOND GRADING REPORT

At the time of writing of this book the GIA Gem Trade Laboratory, Inc., policy is not to grade the quality of the cut or make of a diamond in their Diamond Grading Report. They simply measure some of the physical dimensions of the stone, the largest and smallest diameter and the depth, and describe the ratio of the major physical features of a diamond, namely the depth and table percentage. Therefore it is necessary for you to use the facts available to determine the quality of the cut of the diamond. In my opinion, the key to determining whether a diamond is poorly cut lies in the characteristics of the girdle. If the girdle is described as either extremely thick or extremely thin and the table percentage is above 67.1 percent (large table) or below 53 percent (small table), the stone is poorly cut. Even though the depth percentage may fall within an acceptable range the stone will be poorly proportioned because of the extreme girdle and an oversized crown or pavilion. The following illustrations demonstrate this point:

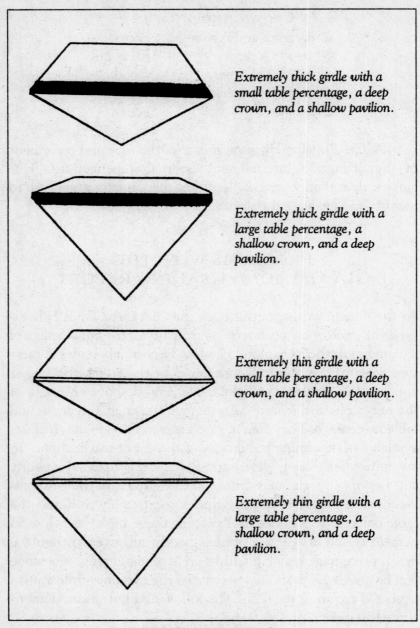

Extremely thick girdle with a small table percentage, a deep crown, and a shallow pavilion.

Extremely thick girdle with a large table percentage, a shallow crown, and a deep pavilion.

Extremely thin girdle with a small table percentage, a deep crown, and a shallow pavilion.

Extremely thin girdle with a large table percentage, a shallow crown, and a deep pavilion.

Poorly Cut Diamonds

There are other proportion problems that can affect the quality of the make or cut of a diamond. For example, the proportions of the crown or pavilion may be too shallow or too deep even if the girdle is not extremely thick or thin. These problems will be difficult to determine unless the stone is visually inspected by an expert because the GIA Diamond Grading Report does not typically describe the crown angles, crown height percentage, and pavilion depth percentage of a diamond.

SPECIAL CONSIDERATIONS USED FOR FANCY-SHAPE DIAMONDS

Even though the proportions for fancy-shape diamonds are not as critical as they are for round, brilliant-cut diamonds, there do exist length-to-width ratios that are considered "standard." Departures from these "standard" ratios may result in significant reductions in value. The following length-to-width ratios represent allowable fluctuations:

Emerald-cut	1.50:1 to 1.75:1
Marquise	1.75:1 to 2.25:1
Oval	1.50:1 to 1.75:1
Pear	1.50:1 to 1.75:1

To more clearly understand the significance of these ratios let us examine an emerald-shaped diamond as an illustration. If a GIA Diamond Grading Report described the length of an emerald-cut diamond as 17 millimeters and the width as 10 millimeters, the length-to-width ratio would be 17 to 10, or 1.70 to 1.00. This would be within the permissible range for this shape stone. If the measurements of another emerald-shaped diamond were 30 millimeters in length and 15 millimeters in width, the length-to-width ratio would be 30 to 15, or 2 to 1. This is an unacceptable ratio; the ratio is too large, and the length of the diamond is too long for its width.

If a fancy-shape diamond falls outside the acceptable ranges of the length-to-width ratios that stone should sell at a discount. Even though you might find this type of diamond personally attractive, failing to adhere to the tolerances of the length-to-width ratio is considered a flaw in the proportions of the diamond and must be considered when determining value.

CHAPTER 9

Rapaport Diamond Report

In this chapter I am going to disclose one of the most closely guarded secrets of the jewelry industry. After I reveal this secret the mystery surrounding diamond prices will disappear forever. You will be able to determine the wholesale price of any diamond and purchase your stone at the best possible price. To my knowledge, I am the first one to publicly disclose this information.

There is a company headquartered in New York City that monitors the wholesale prices of diamonds. Using their contacts throughout the diamond world, they compile the New York cash asking price for GIA-graded certified diamonds of various shapes, sizes, and qualities. Every month this company publishes a comprehensive list that reports the wholesale prices of fancy-shape diamonds. The round, brilliant-cut diamond list is published weekly. This comprehensive index is known as the Rapaport Diamond Report and it has become the industry standard when referring to wholesale diamond prices. Most diamond merchants, jewelry manufacturers, and retailers subscribe to this list, which is also known as the Rap-sheet, or Rap-Report. The prices reflected in this report are the New York cash asking prices for the month prior to the date of the report.

The following pages are reprints of the Rapaport Diamond Report dated February 7, 1997.

RAPAPORT DIAMOND REPORT

Tel: 212-354-0575 ✦ Fax: 212-840-0243 Trd: 212-302-8046 ✦ 15 W 47 St. New York, NY 10036 ✦ Internet: www.diamonds.net
February 7, 1997: Volume 20 No. 6: APPROXIMATE HIGH CASH ASKING PRICE INDICATIONS: Page 33
SPOT CASH NEW YORK: Round Brilliant Cut "Per RDC Spec A" Diamonds in Hundreds US$ Per Carat
THIS IS NOT AN OFFERING TO SELL. THEY REFLECT OUR OPINION OF NEW YORK ASKING PRICES.

News: De Beers and Russia intensify negotiations this week in Moscow. According to CSO president Anthony Oppenheimer it may be "possible for De Beers to sign the new contract by the end of February." However he cautioned that "there could be an awful lot of possibilities in Russia. You can never be certain of the outcome." Cutting centers are still quiet with relatively low transaction volumes. Prices for better goods are firm but demand is not up to expectations.

RAPAPORT: (.01—.03 CT.): 2/7/97 ROUNDS RAPAPORT: (.04—.07 CT.): 2/7/97

	IF-VVS	VS	SI1	SI2	SI3	I1	I2	I3	IF-VVS	VS	SI1	SI2	SI3	I1	I2	I3
D–F	9.1	8.0	7.4	6.8	6.2	5.6	4.8	2.7	9.1	8.0	7.4	6.8	6.4	5.8	5.0	2.7
G–H	8.0	7.4	7.0	6.5	5.8	5.3	4.4	2.5	8.0	7.4	7.0	6.5	6.0	5.5	4.6	2.5
I–J	7.4	7.0	6.5	6.0	5.3	4.8	4.0	2.2	7.4	7.0	6.5	6.0	5.5	5.0	4.2	2.2
K–L	5.9	5.5	4.9	4.4	4.0	3.7	3.2	1.9	6.4	5.9	5.3	4.8	4.4	4.0	3.4	2.0
M–N	4.7	4.3	3.8	3.3	3.1	2.8	2.5	1.7	5.1	4.7	4.0	3.6	3.3	3.0	2.7	1.9

RAPAPORT: (.08—.14 CT.): 2/7/97 ROUNDS RAPAPORT: (.15—.17 CT.): 2/7/97

	IF-VVS	VS	SI1	SI2	SI3	I1	I2	I3	IF-VVS	VS	SI1	SI2	SI3	I1	I2	I3
D–F	10.3	8.8	8.0	7.6	6.7	6.0	5.2	3.0	12.0	10.0	9.0	8.2	7.2	6.4	5.6	3.3
G–H	8.8	8.0	7.6	7.0	6.3	5.7	4.8	2.8	10.0	9.0	8.5	7.7	6.7	6.1	5.2	3.0
I–J	8.0	7.5	6.8	6.4	5.8	5.2	4.4	2.5	9.0	8.5	8.0	7.1	6.3	5.8	4.8	2.8
K–L	7.0	6.4	5.7	5.2	4.8	4.5	3.6	2.3	7.6	6.7	6.0	5.0	4.7	4.0	2.6	
M–N	5.6	5.2	4.4	3.9	3.5	3.2	2.9	2.2	6.5	6.2	5.7	4.5	4.1	3.8	3.4	2.4

RAPAPORT: (.18—.22 CT.): 2/7/97 ROUNDS RAPAPORT: (.23—.29 CT.): 2/7/97

	F-VVS	VS	SI1	SI2	SI3	I1	I2	I3	IF-VVS	VS	SI1	SI2	SI3	I1	I2	I3
D–F	14.0	12.0	11.5	10.0	9.0	8.0	6.8	4.2	21.0	16.0	12.5	11.0	9.6	8.6	7.7	5.1
G–H	11.7	11.5	10.5	9.5	8.5	7.7	6.5	3.8	16.0	14.5	11.5	10.5	9.3	8.3	7.5	4.9
I–J	11.0	10.5	9.5	8.7	7.5	7.0	5.6	3.4	13.0	12.0	10.5	9.8	8.6	7.8	6.5	4.3
K–L	9.5	9.0	8.5	7.5	6.5	6.0	5.0	3.2	11.0	10.0	9.5	9.0	8.0	7.5	6.0	3.8
M–N	7.6	7.4	6.7	6.0	5.5	5.0	4.5	3.0	9.0	8.5	8.0	7.0	6.5	6.0	5.0	3.5

RAPAPORT: (.30—.37 CT.): 2/7/97 ROUNDS RAPAPORT: (.38—.45 CT.): 2/7/97

	IF	VVS1	VVS2	VS1	VS2	SI1	SI2	SI3	I1	I2	I3	IF	VVS1	VVS2	VS1	VS2	SI1	SI2	SI3	I1	I2	I3
D	50	47	44	36	28	21	19	17	14	11	8	53	50	45	37	31	24	22	20	16	12	9
E	47	44	39	34	26	20	18	17	13	10	7	50	47	43	35	29	23	21	19	15	11	8
F	44	39	36	31	25	19	17	16	12	9	7	47	43	39	32	28	23	20	18	15	11	8
G	38	35	31	28	23	18	16	15	11	9	6	41	37	34	29	27	22	19	17	14	10	7
H	29	27	25	23	19	17	15	14	10	8	6	32	29	27	25	23	20	18	16	13	10	7
I	22	21	20	19	17	16	14	13	10	8	6	26	25	24	23	21	18	16	15	12	9	7
J	20	19	18	17	15	14	13	12	9	8	5	23	22	20	18	17	16	14	13	11	9	6
K	17	16	15	14	13	12	11	10	9	7	5	20	19	18	16	15	14	13	12	10	8	6
L	15	14	14	13	12	11	10	8	7	6	4	19	18	16	15	14	13	12	10	9	7	5
M	13	13	12	11	10	9	8	7	6	5	4	16	15	14	13	12	11	10	9	8	6	4

W: 33.92 = 0.00% ✦✦✦ T: 17.32 = 0.00% W: 36.52 = 0.00% ✦✦✦ T: 19.57 = 0.00%

RAPAPORT: (.46—.49 CT.): 2/7/97 ROUNDS RAPAPORT: (.50—.69 CT.): 2/7/97

	IF	VVS1	VVS2	VS1	VS2	SI1	SI2	SI3	I1	I2	I3	IF	VVS1	VVS2	VS1	VS2	SI1	SI2	SI3	I1	I2	I3
D	56	53	48	41	34	27	24	22	18	13	10	81	66	60	50	41	35	28	25	21	15	11
E	53	50	46	38	32	26	23	21	17	13	10	66	61	52	47	40	34	27	24	20	14	10
F	50	46	42	35	30	25	22	20	16	12	9	61	53	47	44	38	32	26	23	19	13	10
G	43	39	36	31	28	24	21	19	15	12	9	53	47	43	41	36	30	25	22	18	13	9
H	35	33	31	27	25	22	19	18	14	11	9	45	41	37	35	31	28	23	20	17	12	9
I	31	29	27	25	23	20	18	17	13	11	9	36	33	31	28	26	24	22	19	16	12	9
J	24	23	22	21	20	18	16	15	12	11	8	30	28	26	25	24	23	21	18	15	12	8
K	22	20	19	17	16	15	14	13	11	10	8	24	23	22	21	20	19	17	16	14	11	8
L	20	18	17	16	15	14	13	11	10	9	7	23	22	21	20	19	18	16	14	11	10	7
M	17	16	15	14	13	12	11	10	9	8	6	20	19	18	17	16	15	14	12	10	9	6

W: 39.28 = 0.00% ✦✦✦ T: 21.47 = 0.00% W: 48.64 = 0.00% ✦✦✦ T: 25.88 = 0.00%

Rapaport Diamond Report. Reprinted courtesy of Rapaport Diamond Report.

RAPAPORT DIAMOND REPORT

Tel: 212-354-0575 ✦ Fax: 212-840-0243 ✦ 15 West 47th Street, New York, NY 10036 ✦ Internet: www.diamonds.net
February 7, 1997: Volume 20 No. 6: APPROXIMATE CASH ASKING PRICE INDICATIONS: Page 34
SPOT CASH N.Y.: Round Diamonds in Hundreds US$ Per Carat: THIS IS NOT AN OFFERING TO SELL.

We grade SI-3 as a split SI2/I1 clarity. Price changes are in **Bold.** Price decreases are in *Italics.* 1.75–1.99 and all stones close to higher sizes (0.95–0.99 through 5.90–5.95) bring better prices.

RAPAPORT: (.70—.89 CT.): 2/7/97 — ROUNDS

	IF	VVS1	VVS2	VS1	VS2	SI1	SI2	SI3	I1	I2	I3
D	88	70	63	55	49	45	40	34	27	18	12
E	70	65	56	51	47	44	39	32	26	18	11
F	64	57	51	48	45	43	38	31	26	17	11
G	56	51	48	45	43	40	36	30	25	17	10
H	50	46	44	42	40	37	34	28	24	16	10
I	43	41	39	37	36	34	30	26	23	15	10
J	37	36	35	33	31	29	27	23	22	14	9
K	33	32	31	29	27	25	23	20	18	13	9
L	27	26	25	24	23	22	20	16	13	11	8
M	25	24	23	22	21	20	18	15	12	10	7

W: 53.76 = 0.00% ✦✦✦ T: 31.50 = 0.00%

RAPAPORT: (.90—.99 CT.): 2/7/97 — ROUNDS

	IF	VVS1	VVS2	VS1	VS2	SI1	SI2	SI3	I1	I2	I3
D	95	75	70	62	56	50	45	38	32	24	14
E	75	70	62	56	53	49	44	37	31	23	13
F	70	62	56	53	50	47	42	36	30	22	13
G	62	56	53	50	48	45	40	34	29	21	12
H	55	52	50	48	46	43	38	32	28	20	12
I	49	47	45	43	41	39	35	31	27	19	11
J	44	42	40	38	36	34	31	28	26	18	11
K	38	37	36	34	32	30	27	25	21	16	10
L	31	30	29	28	27	26	24	22	18	14	9
M	29	28	27	26	25	24	22	20	17	13	9

W: 59.40 = 0.00% ✦✦✦ T: 36.07 = 0.00%

RAPAPORT: (1.00—1.49 CT.): 2/7/97 — ROUNDS

	IF	VVS1	VVS2	VS1	VS2	SI1	SI2	SI3	I1	I2	I3
D	164	111	96	78	68	60	54	43	35	24	15
E	111	98	79	72	66	59	53	42	34	24	14
F	97	80	72	69	64	58	51	41	33	23	14
G	79	72	68	65	61	56	49	39	32	22	13
H	69	66	63	60	57	53	47	38	31	21	13
I	61	58	55	53	50	47	42	37	30	19	12
J	54	52	50	48	46	42	38	33	28	18	12
K	49	47	46	44	41	39	35	31	26	17	11
L	43	42	40	38	36	34	31	28	24	16	10
M	35	34	33	31	29	27	25	23	19	15	10

W: 79.40 = 0.00% ✦✦✦ T: 45.17 = 0.00%

RAPAPORT: (1.50—1.99 CT.): 2/7/97 — ROUNDS

	IF	VVS1	VVS2	VS1	VS2	SI1	SI2	SI3	I1	I2	I3
D	180	122	111	93	82	73	62	50	39	28	16
E	122	112	96	89	80	71	61	49	38	27	15
F	112	96	89	84	78	69	59	48	37	26	15
G	95	87	82	78	74	66	56	46	36	25	14
H	80	76	73	70	67	61	52	44	35	24	14
I	69	67	65	63	60	54	48	42	34	23	13
J	62	60	58	56	52	48	43	38	32	22	13
K	55	53	51	49	46	43	39	35	29	20	12
L	47	45	43	41	39	37	34	31	26	19	11
M	40	39	38	36	33	30	28	26	22	17	11

W: 93.12 = 0.00% ✦✦✦ T: 52.10 = 0.00%

RAPAPORT: (2.00—2.99 CT.): 2/7/97 — ROUNDS

	IF	VVS1	VVS2	VS1	VS2	SI1	SI2	SI3	I1	I2	I3
D	260	192	168	133	107	88	72	57	43	31	18
E	192	168	134	117	103	86	70	55	42	30	17
F	167	134	118	106	99	84	68	54	41	29	16
G	133	118	104	99	93	80	66	53	40	28	16
H	113	99	93	88	82	72	61	50	39	27	15
I	88	85	81	76	71	63	55	47	38	26	14
J	75	72	69	64	60	54	49	44	37	24	14
K	62	60	58	56	53	49	45	41	34	23	13
L	53	51	49	47	44	41	38	34	30	22	12
M	45	43	41	38	36	33	31	29	25	20	12

W: 128.80 = 0.00% ✦✦✦ T: 64.93 = 0.00%

RAPAPORT: (3.00—3.99 CT.): 2/7/97 — ROUNDS

	IF	VVS1	VVS2	VS1	VS2	SI1	SI2	SI3	I1	I2	I3
D	403	285	241	187	152	124	92	79	68	37	20
E	285	241	187	152	135	116	87	75	63	36	19
F	241	187	152	135	125	108	83	71	59	34	18
G	186	152	135	126	110	96	78	67	56	32	17
H	150	132	122	110	96	82	73	62	52	30	17
I	117	107	102	94	80	73	64	56	48	29	16
J	97	92	88	80	72	66	59	52	44	27	15
K	86	82	77	70	64	58	51	46	41	25	15
L	70	67	63	58	53	47	41	37	32	24	14
M	57	55	53	49	46	41	36	33	28	22	14

W: 177.08 = 0.00% ✦✦✦ T: 84.65 = 0.00%

RAPAPORT: (4.00—4.99 CT.): 2/7/97 — ROUNDS

	IF	VVS1	VVS2	VS1	VS2	SI1	SI2	SI3	I1	I2	I3
D	422	307	261	202	167	137	99	86	74	42	21
E	307	262	202	167	148	127	93	81	69	41	20
F	262	202	167	147	137	117	89	76	65	39	19
G	202	167	147	137	118	102	85	72	61	37	18
H	161	146	131	118	102	91	78	67	57	35	18
I	126	116	108	102	94	81	72	63	54	33	17
J	100	95	90	85	80	71	65	57	49	31	16
K	88	84	80	74	68	61	56	50	44	28	15
L	71	68	65	62	57	51	45	41	36	26	14
M	59	57	55	53	50	45	40	36	32	24	14

W: 191.56 = 0.00% ✦✦✦ T: 91.45 = 0.00%

RAPAPORT: (5.00—5.99 CT.): 2/7/97 — ROUNDS

	IF	VVS1	VVS2	VS1	VS2	SI1	SI2	SI3	I1	I2	I3
D	562	393	335	278	228	192	132	107	81	47	24
E	393	338	278	238	207	172	127	101	76	45	22
F	338	278	243	212	182	152	122	97	73	43	21
G	277	243	212	182	159	139	114	92	69	41	20
H	232	206	182	159	140	119	98	82	64	39	19
I	181	171	159	138	122	98	86	72	58	37	18
J	127	122	117	112	98	82	73	63	53	35	17
K	101	97	92	87	81	72	61	55	48	32	17
L	83	78	74	69	64	59	51	47	42	29	16
M	65	62	59	55	51	46	41	36	26	16	

W: 259.80 = 0.00% ✦✦✦ T: 117.67 = 0.00%

* 0.60–0.69: 0.96–0.99: 1.30–1.49: 1.75–1.99: 2.50–2.99: May be 5–10% over straight sizes.

RAPAPORT DIAMOND REPORT

Tel: 212-354-0575 ✦ Fax: 212-840-0243 ✦ 15 West 47th Street, New York, NY 10036 ✦ Internet: www.diamonds.net
February 7, 1997: Volume 20 No. 6: APPROXIMATE HIGH CASH ASKING PRICE INDICATIONS: Page 35

PEAR SHAPES SPOT CASH-NY-FINE CUT, IN HUNDRED U.S.$ PER CARAT.

The *Rapaport Diamond Report* is pleased to announce that we have begun publishing monthly prices for Marquise and Emerald Cut diamonds. Trade discounts for these price sheets are similar to the discounts for the round price sheet.

APPROXIMATE CONVERSION SCALE FOR OTHER SHAPES.

Radiant: As Emerald Cut prices with possibility of 3% to 5% premiums.
Princess: Better than Emerald Cut prices with 3% to 5% premiums.
Hearts & Ovals: As Pear Shape prices with possibility of up to 3% labor premium for small stones and 0 to 5% discount for larger sizes. Market demand and availability is volatile.

News: Overall demand is low and market is very quiet for this time of year. In spite of soft market fine makes are still very expensive and in limited supply. Large stones are doing well, especially Princess, Radiants and Emerald Cuts. Better color 6/5 to 7/4 SI's are very strong with shortages limiting trading activity. U.S. Valentine's day holiday should help boost short term demand for medium quality smaller heart shapes. Hong Kong market more active but Japan very slow due to very high Yen rate.

RAPAPORT: (.18—.22 CT.): 2/7/97   PEARS   RAPAPORT: (.23—.29 CT.): 2/7/97

	IF-VVS	VS	SI1	SI2	SI3	I1	I2	I3	IF-VVS	VS	SI1	SI2	SI3	I1	I2	I3
D–F	12.0	10.0	9.0	8.0	7.5	6.7	5.5	4.0	15.0	13.0	10.0	9.0	8.0	7.3	6.0	4.5
G–H	10.0	9.0	8.0	7.5	7.0	6.4	5.2	3.5	13.0	10.5	9.0	8.0	7.5	7.1	5.5	4.0
I–J	8.8	8.0	7.5	7.0	6.5	6.0	4.8	3.0	10.5	9.5	8.3	7.5	7.2	6.7	5.0	3.5
K–L	7.5	7.0	6.5	5.8	5.5	5.0	4.0	2.6	9.0	8.5	7.5	6.6	6.3	6.0	4.5	3.0
M–N	6.6	5.5	5.0	4.5	4.2	3.9	3.4	2.2	7.5	6.5	5.5	5.0	4.6	4.2	3.7	2.6

PEARS : PEARS : PEARS : PEARS : PEARS : PEARS : PEARS : PEARS : PEARS : PEARS : PEARS : PEARS : PEARS : PEARS : PEARS : PEARS
*It is illegal and unethical to reproduce this price sheet. Please do not make copies.©1997

RAPAPORT: (.30—.37 CT.): 2/7/97   PEARS   RAPAPORT: (.38—.45 CT.): 2/7/97

	IF	VVS1	VVS2	VS1	VS2	SI1	SI2	SI3	I1	I2	I3	IF	VVS1	VVS2	VS1	VS2	SI1	SI2	SI3	I1	I2	I3
D	33	31	29	27	23	20	17	15	13	10	7	37	35	33	30	26	23	21	18	14	11	9
E	31	29	27	23	20	19	17	15	12	9	6	35	33	31	28	25	22	20	17	13	10	8
F	29	27	24	21	19	18	16	15	11	8	6	33	31	28	26	24	21	19	16	12	9	7
G	27	24	22	20	18	17	15	14	10	8	5	31	28	26	24	22	20	17	15	11	9	7
H	22	21	20	19	17	16	14	13	9	7	5	27	25	23	22	21	19	16	14	10	8	6
I	18	17	16	16	15	14	13	12	9	7	4	22	21	20	19	17	16	14	13	10	8	6
J	16	15	15	14	13	12	10	10	8	6	4	19	18	18	17	15	14	12	11	9	7	5
K	14	13	12	12	11	10	9	8	7	5	4	17	16	15	14	13	12	10	9	8	6	5
L	12	11	11	10	10	9	8	7	5	4	3	14	13	13	12	11	10	9	8	6	5	4
M	10	10	10	9	9	8	7	6	5	3	3	11	11	11	10	10	9	8	7	6	4	4

PEARS   PEARS   PEARS   PEARS   PEARS   PEARS   PEARS   PEARS   PEARS   PEARS   PEARS   PEARS

RAPAPORT: (.46—.49 CT.): 2/7/97   PEARS   RAPAPORT: (.50—.69 CT.): 2/7/97

	IF	VVS1	VVS2	VS1	VS2	SI1	SI2	SI3	I1	I2	I3	IF	VVS1	VVS2	VS1	VS2	SI1	SI2	SI3	I1	I2	I3
D	41	37	35	33	30	26	23	20	17	13	10	57	50	46	41	36	31	27	24	20	15	11
E	37	35	33	31	29	25	22	19	17	13	9	50	46	41	36	33	30	26	23	19	14	10
F	35	33	31	29	28	24	21	19	16	12	9	46	41	36	33	31	29	25	22	18	13	10
G	33	31	30	28	26	23	20	18	15	12	8	41	36	33	31	29	27	24	21	17	13	9
H	29	28	27	25	23	21	18	17	14	11	8	36	33	31	29	27	25	23	20	16	12	9
I	25	24	23	22	21	19	17	15	13	11	7	32	29	28	26	25	24	22	19	15	12	8
J	22	21	20	19	18	17	14	13	12	10	7	26	25	24	23	22	21	19	17	14	11	8
K	18	17	16	15	14	13	13	12	11	9	6	20	19	19	18	17	16	15	12	10	7	
L	15	14	14	13	12	11	10	9	8	7	6	17	16	16	15	15	14	13	12	9	8	7
M	12	12	12	11	11	10	9	8	7	6	5	14	14	14	13	13	12	11	10	8	7	6

PEARS   PEARS   PEARS   PEARS   PEARS   PEARS   PEARS   PEARS   PEARS   PEARS   PEARS   PEARS

RAPAPORT DIAMOND REPORT

Tel: 212-354-0575 ✦ Fax: 212-840-0243 ✦ 15 West 47th Street, New York, NY 10036 ✦ Internet: www.diamonds.net
February 7, 1997: Volume 20 No. 6: APPROXIMATE HIGH CASH ASKING PRICE INDICATIONS Page 36
SPOT CASH N.Y.: Pear Shape Diamonds in Hundreds US$ Per Carat: THIS IS NOT AN OFFERING TO SELL.

We grade SI-3 as a split SI2/SI1 clarity. Price changes are in **Bold**. Price decreases are *italicized*.
Prices for fancy shapes are highly dependent on the cut. Poorly made stones often trade at huge
discounts while well-made stones may be hard to locate and bring premium prices.

RAPAPORT: (.70—.89 CT.): 2/7/97 — PEARS

	IF	VVS1	VVS2	VS1	VS2	SI1	SI2	SI3	I1	I2	I3
D	74	59	55	51	47	43	37	31	24	17	12
E	59	55	51	49	46	42	36	30	23	17	11
F	55	51	49	47	45	41	35	29	22	16	11
G	51	49	47	45	43	39	34	28	21	16	10
H	47	45	44	42	40	37	31	26	20	15	10
I	41	40	39	38	36	34	28	24	19	14	9
J	35	34	33	32	31	29	25	21	17	13	9
K	29	28	27	26	25	23	21	19	15	12	8
L	24	23	22	21	20	19	18	16	12	10	8
M	17	17	17	16	16	15	14	13	9	8	7

RAPAPORT: (.90—.99 CT.): 2/7/97 — PEARS

	IF	VVS1	VVS2	VS1	VS2	SI1	SI2	SI3	I1	I2	I3
D	83	64	61	56	52	46	40	34	27	20	13
E	64	61	56	53	50	45	39	33	26	20	12
F	56	53	50	48	44	38	32	26	19	12	11
G	56	53	51	49	46	43	37	31	25	18	11
H	52	49	47	45	43	40	34	30	24	18	11
I	46	44	42	40	38	37	32	27	23	17	10
J	40	39	38	36	34	32	28	25	21	15	10
K	32	31	30	29	28	26	24	22	18	13	9
L	26	25	24	23	22	21	20	18	14	11	9
M	19	19	18	18	17	17	16	15	10	9	8

PEARS : PEARS : PEARS : PEARS : PEARS : PEARS : PEARS : PEARS : PEARS : PEARS : PEARS : PEARS

RAPAPORT: (1.00—1.49 CT.): 2/7/97 — PEARS

	IF	VVS1	VVS2	VS1	VS2	SI1	SI2	SI3	I1	I2	I3
D	127	82	72	68	64	55	46	39	31	23	14
E	82	72	68	65	62	53	45	38	30	22	13
F	72	68	65	62	58	51	44	37	29	22	13
G	67	64	61	58	55	49	43	36	28	21	12
H	63	59	56	53	50	46	41	34	27	20	11
I	54	52	50	48	45	42	37	32	26	19	11
J	45	43	41	39	37	35	32	27	23	16	11
K	38	37	36	35	33	31	28	24	21	14	10
L	32	31	30	29	27	25	23	20	17	12	9
M	25	25	24	24	22	20	18	17	13	11	8

RAPAPORT: (1.50—1.99 CT.): 2/7/97 — PEARS

	IF	VVS1	VVS2	VS1	VS2	SI1	SI2	SI3	I1	I2	I3
D	142	92	82	77	73	65	55	45	35	25	14
E	92	82	77	73	70	63	54	44	34	24	14
F	77	73	70	67	60	52	43	33	23	13	13
G	71	69	66	63	57	50	42	32	22	13	13
H	68	65	62	59	56	51	45	40	31	21	12
I	58	56	54	51	49	45	41	37	29	20	12
J	50	49	47	45	43	40	36	31	26	18	11
K	42	41	40	38	36	34	31	27	23	16	11
L	35	34	33	32	30	28	25	22	19	15	8
M	28	28	27	26	24	22	20	19	15	13	8

PEARS : PEARS : PEARS : PEARS : PEARS : PEARS : PEARS : PEARS : PEARS : PEARS : PEARS : PEARS : PEARS : PEARS : PEARS

RAPAPORT: (2.00—2.99 CT.): 2/7/97 — PEARS

	IF	VVS1	VVS2	VS1	VS2	SI1	SI2	SI3	I1	I2	I3
D	212	143	129	115	105	82	62	52	41	27	16
E	143	129	115	107	94	79	60	49	39	26	15
F	129	115	107	94	88	75	58	47	37	24	15
G	115	107	94	88	81	69	55	45	35	23	14
H	107	93	82	77	69	61	50	42	33	22	13
I	82	77	72	65	59	53	46	39	30	21	13
J	64	61	58	54	49	45	39	34	28	20	12
K	52	49	47	45	42	39	35	30	25	19	12
L	42	40	38	36	33	31	29	25	21	17	11
M	34	33	31	30	28	26	24	22	18	15	9

RAPAPORT: (3.00—3.99 CT.): 2/7/97 — PEARS

	IF	VVS1	VVS2	VS1	VS2	SI1	SI2	SI3	I1	I2	I3
D	297	214	184	164	144	122	85	78	67	35	20
E	214	184	164	144	131	114	80	73	62	33	19
F	184	164	144	131	122	105	76	68	58	31	18
G	164	144	131	122	106	92	73	64	55	29	17
H	142	130	115	106	92	77	70	60	50	27	16
I	115	105	100	92	77	70	60	53	45	25	15
J	86	81	76	71	66	58	50	44	37	23	14
K	69	66	62	57	54	49	42	38	33	21	13
L	54	52	49	46	44	39	35	31	27	19	12
M	53	37	36	34	32	29	26	24	22	18	10

PEARS : PEARS : PEARS : PEARS : PEARS : PEARS : PEARS : PEARS : PEARS : PEARS : PEARS

RAPAPORT: (4.00—4.99 CT.): 2/7/97 — PEARS

	IF	VVS1	VVS2	VS1	VS2	SI1	SI2	SI3	I1	I2	I3
D	315	229	199	179	159	132	95	85	73	40	21
E	229	199	179	159	142	125	90	80	68	37	20
F	199	179	159	142	129	115	86	76	64	35	19
G	179	159	140	129	115	100	82	70	60	33	18
H	154	140	125	115	100	90	75	66	56	31	17
I	120	110	105	100	90	80	65	57	48	29	16
J	91	86	81	76	71	65	55	49	42	27	15
K	74	70	66	63	59	55	50	44	38	24	14
L	59	57	55	52	50	45	38	35	31	22	13
M	46	44	42	40	38	35	30	27	25	20	11

RAPAPORT: (5.00—5.99 CT.): 2/7/97 — PEARS

	IF	VVS1	VVS2	VS1	VS2	SI1	SI2	SI3	I1	I2	I3
D	445	310	280	250	225	185	125	105	80	44	24
E	309	280	250	225	203	170	120	100	75	42	22
F	279	250	225	203	176	150	115	95	72	40	20
G	249	225	200	176	155	135	110	90	68	38	19
H	215	195	170	155	135	115	95	80	62	36	17
I	157	147	142	130	115	95	80	70	57	34	17
J	115	110	105	100	90	80	70	62	52	31	16
K	92	88	85	80	75	70	60	54	47	28	15
L	71	69	68	66	62	57	48	46	42	25	14
M	53	51	49	47	45	42	38	34	30	22	13

PEARS : PEARS : PEARS : PEARS : PEARS : PEARS : PEARS : PEARS : PEARS : PEARS : PEARS

* 0.60–0.69: 0.96–0.99: 1.30–1.49: 1.75–1.99: 2.50–2.99: May be 5–10% over straight sizes. Severe shortages of well made 3/4's and 7/4's.

RAPAPORT DIAMOND REPORT

Tel: 212-354-0575 ✦ Fax: 212-840-0243 ✦ 15 West 47th Street, New York, NY 10036 ✦ Internet: www.diamonds.net
February 7, 1997: Volume 20 No. 6: APPROXIMATE HIGH CASH ASKING PRICE INDICATIONS: Page 37

Marquise SPOT CASH-NY-FINE CUT, IN HUNDRED U.S.$ PER CARAT.

The *Rapaport Diamond Report* is pleased to announce that we have begun publishing monthly prices for Marquise and Emerald Cut diamonds. Trade discounts for these price sheets are similar to the discounts for the round price sheets.

Notice: Fancy shape diamonds are more complex than round diamonds and much harder to valuate. The quality of cut, proportions, and the overall shape of the fancy shape diamond all have a great impact on price and liquidity. Poorly cut stones may trade at substantial discounts, while well-shaped fine cut stones may trade at a premium. There is also a higher degree of availability difficulties in the fancy market and you may have to pay significantly higher prices for a select fine stone. Matching stones may also require a premium. It is not advisable to trade diamonds solely on the basis of the grading report. All stones should be examined by an expert. Consumers are cautioned to consult with a reputable jeweler to avoid buying a poorly cut, treated or misrepresented diamond. These price indications should only be used as a general guideline. Prices vary. This price sheet is not an offering to sell.

Prices for Fine Cut Stones Only. Medium and Poorly Cut stones may trade at very large discounts.

RAPAPORT: (.18—.22 CT.): 2/7/97   MARQUISE   RAPAPORT: (.23—.29 CT.): 2/7/97

	IF-VVS	VS	SI1	SI2	SI3	I1	I2	I3	IF-VVS	VS	SI1	SI2	SI3	I1	I2	I3
D–F	13.0	11.0	10.0	9.0	8.5	7.7	6.3	4.6	16.0	14.0	11.0	10.0	9.0	8.3	6.9	5.2
G–H	11.0	10.0	9.0	8.5	8.0	7.4	6.0	4.0	14.0	11.5	10.0	9.0	8.5	8.1	6.3	4.6
I–J	10.0	9.0	8.5	8.0	7.5	6.9	5.5	3.5	11.5	10.5	9.3	8.5	8.2	7.7	5.8	4.0
K–L	8.5	8.0	7.5	6.7	6.3	5.8	4.6	3.0	10.0	9.5	8.5	7.6	7.2	6.9	5.2	3.5
M–N	7.6	6.3	5.8	5.2	4.8	4.5	3.9	2.5	8.5	7.5	6.3	5.8	5.3	4.8	4.3	3.0

MARQUISE : MARQUISE : MARQUISE : MARQUISE : MARQUISE : MARQUISE : MARQUISE : MARQUISE : MARQUISE : MARQUISE : MARQUISE
*It is illegal and unethical to reproduce this price sheet. Please do not make copies. ©1997

RAPAPORT: (.30—.37 CT.): 2/7/97   MARQUISE   RAPAPORT: (.38—.45 CT.): 2/7/97

	IF	VVS1	VVS2	VS1	VS2	SI1	SI2	SI3	I1	I2	I3	IF	VVS1	VVS2	VS1	VS2	SI1	SI2	SI3	I1	I2	I3
D	33	31	29	27	23	20	17	15	13	10	7	37	35	33	30	26	24	21	18	14	11	9
E	31	29	27	23	20	19	17	15	12	9	6	35	33	31	28	25	23	20	17	13	10	8
F	29	27	24	21	19	18	16	15	11	8	6	33	31	28	26	24	22	19	16	12	9	7
G	27	24	22	20	18	17	15	14	10	8	5	31	28	26	24	23	21	18	15	11	9	7
H	22	21	20	19	17	16	14	13	9	7	5	27	25	23	22	21	19	16	14	10	8	6
I	18	17	16	16	15	14	13	12	9	7	4	22	21	20	19	17	16	14	13	10	8	6
J	16	15	15	14	13	12	10	10	8	6	4	19	18	18	17	15	14	12	11	9	7	5
K	14	13	12	12	11	10	9	8	7	5	4	17	16	15	14	13	12	10	9	8	6	5
L	12	11	11	10	10	9	8	7	5	4	3	14	13	13	12	11	10	9	8	6	5	4
M	11	10	10	9	9	8	7	6	4	3	3	12	11	11	10	10	9	8	7	6	4	4

MARQUISE MARQUISE MARQUISE MARQUISE MARQUISE MARQUISE MARQUISE MARQUISE MARQUISE MARQUISE

RAPAPORT: (.46—.49 CT.): 2/7/97   MARQUISE   RAPAPORT: (.50—.69 CT.): 2/7/97

	IF	VVS1	VVS2	VS1	VS2	SI1	SI2	SI3	I1	I2	I3	IF	VVS1	VVS2	VS1	VS2	SI1	SI2	SI3	I1	I2	I3
D	41	37	35	33	30	27	24	21	17	13	10	57	50	46	41	36	31	27	24	20	15	11
E	37	35	33	31	29	26	23	20	17	13	9	50	46	41	37	34	31	26	23	19	14	10
F	35	33	31	29	28	25	22	19	16	12	9	46	41	36	34	32	30	25	22	18	13	10
G	33	31	30	28	26	24	21	18	15	12	8	41	36	33	32	30	28	24	21	17	13	9
H	29	28	27	25	23	22	19	17	14	11	8	36	33	31	30	28	26	23	20	16	12	9
I	25	24	23	22	21	20	18	15	13	11	7	32	29	28	27	26	25	22	19	15	12	8
J	22	21	20	19	18	17	14	13	12	10	7	26	25	24	23	22	20	19	18	14	11	8
K	18	17	16	15	14	13	13	12	11	9	6	20	19	19	18	18	17	16	15	12	10	7
L	15	14	14	13	12	11	10	9	8	7	6	17	16	16	15	15	14	13	12	9	8	7
M	13	12	12	11	11	10	9	8	7	6	5	15	14	14	13	13	12	11	10	8	7	6

MARQUISE MARQUISE MARQUISE MARQUISE MARQUISE MARQUISE MARQUISE MARQUISE MARQUISE MARQUISE

RAPAPORT DIAMOND REPORT

Tel: 212-354-0575 ✦ Fax: 212-840-0243 ✦ 15 West 47th Street, New York, NY 10036 ✦ Internet: www.diamonds.net
February 7, 1997: Volume 20 No. 6: APPROXIMATE HIGH CASH ASKING PRICE INDICATIONS Page 38

SPOT CASH N.Y.: Marquise Shape Diamonds in Hundreds US$ Per Carat: THIS IS NOT AN OFFERING TO SELL.
We grade SI-3 as a split SI2/I1 clarity. Price changes are in **Bold**. Price decreases are *italicized*.
Prices for fancy shapes are highly dependent on the cut. Poorly made stones often trade at huge
discounts while well-made stones may be hard to locate and bring premium prices.

MARQUISE — RAPAPORT: (.70—.89 CT.): 2/7/97

	IF	VVS1	VVS2	VS1	VS2	SI1	SI2	SI3	I1	I2	I3
D	75	61	58	54	50	46	39	33	25	18	12
E	60	57	54	51	49	45	38	32	24	18	12
F	56	53	51	49	48	44	37	30	23	17	11
G	52	51	49	47	46	42	36	29	22	17	10
H	48	47	44	44	42	39	33	28	21	16	10
I	42	41	40	39	37	35	30	26	20	15	9
J	36	35	34	33	32	30	26	22	18	14	9
K	30	29	28	27	26	24	22	20	16	13	8
L	25	24	23	22	21	20	19	16	12	10	7
M	18	17	17	16	16	15	14	13	9	8	6

MARQUISE — RAPAPORT: (.90—.99 CT.): 2/7/97

	IF	VVS1	VVS2	VS1	VS2	SI1	SI2	SI3	I1	I2	I3
D	86	67	64	59	55	49	43	36	28	21	13
E	67	64	59	56	53	48	42	35	27	21	13
F	64	59	56	53	51	47	41	34	27	20	12
G	59	56	54	52	49	46	40	33	26	19	11
H	54	52	50	48	46	43	37	32	25	18	11
I	48	46	44	42	40	39	34	29	24	17	10
J	42	41	40	38	36	34	30	27	22	16	10
K	32	32	31	30	29	27	25	23	19	14	9
L	27	26	25	24	23	22	21	19	15	12	8
M	20	19	18	18	17	17	16	15	10	9	7

MARQUISE MARQUISE MARQUISE MARQUISE MARQUISE MARQUISE MARQUISE MARQUISE MARQUISE MARQUISE MARQUISE

MARQUISE — RAPAPORT: (1.00—1.49 CT.): 2/7/97

	IF	VVS1	VVS2	VS1	VS2	SI1	SI2	SI3	I1	I2	I3
D	127	82	74	71	67	58	49	41	33	24	14
E	82	74	71	68	65	56	48	40	32	23	14
F	74	71	68	65	61	53	47	39	30	23	13
G	69	67	64	61	58	51	46	38	29	22	13
H	65	62	59	56	53	49	44	36	28	21	12
I	56	54	52	50	47	44	39	34	27	20	12
J	47	45	43	41	39	37	34	29	25	18	11
K	39	38	37	36	34	32	29	25	22	15	11
L	33	32	31	30	28	26	24	21	18	13	10
M	26	25	24	24	23	21	19		14	12	8

MARQUISE — RAPAPORT: (1.50—1.99 CT.): 2/7/97

	IF	VVS1	VVS2	VS1	VS2	SI1	SI2	SI3	I1	I2	I3
D	142	92	82	78	75	66	56	47	37	26	15
E	92	82	78	75	73	65	56	46	36	25	15
F	82	78	74	73	70	63	54	45	35	24	14
G	78	74	71	69	66	60	52	44	34	23	14
H	70	68	65	62	59	54	48	43	33	22	13
I	60	58	56	54	52	48	44	40	31	21	13
J	52	49	47	45	42	38	33		27	19	12
K	44	43	42	40	38	36	33	29	25	18	12
L	36	35	34	33	31	29	26	23	20	15	11
M	29	28	27	26	25	23	21	20	16	14	9

MARQUISE : MARQUISE : MARQUISE : MARQUISE : MARQUISE : MARQUISE : MARQUISE : MARQUISE : MARQUISE : MARQUISE : MARQUISE

MARQUISE — RAPAPORT: (2.00—2.99 CT.): 2/7/97

	IF	VVS1	VVS2	VS1	VS2	SI1	SI2	SI3	I1	I2	I3
D	212	143	129	115	107	85	65	54	41	27	16
E	143	129	115	107	97	82	63	51	40	26	16
F	129	115	107	97	91	78	61	49	39	25	15
G	115	107	97	91	84	72	58	47	37	24	15
H	107	96	85	80	72	64	53	44	35	23	14
I	84	79	74	67	62	56	48	41	32	22	14
J	66	63	60	56	52	48	41	36	30	20	13
K	54	51	49	47	44	41	36	31	26	19	13
L	44	42	40	38	34	32	30	25	21	17	12
M	34	32	32	31	29	27	24	22	18	15	10

MARQUISE — RAPAPORT: (3.00—3.99 CT.): 2/7/97

	IF	VVS1	VVS2	VS1	VS2	SI1	SI2	SI3	I1	I2	I3
D	297	214	184	164	144	122	85	78	67	35	20
E	214	184	164	144	141	114	80	73	62	33	19
F	184	164	144	131	122	105	76	68	58	31	18
G	164	144	131	122	106	92	73	64	55	29	17
H	142	130	115	106	92	77	70	60	50	27	16
I	105	100	92		77	70	60	53	45	25	15
J	86	81	76	71	66	58	50	44	37	23	14
K	69	66	62	57	54	49	42	38	33	22	14
L	54	52	49	46	44	39	35	31	27	19	13
M	37	36	34	34	32	29	26	24	22	18	11

MARQUISE MARQUISE MARQUISE MARQUISE MARQUISE MARQUISE MARQUISE MARQUISE MARQUISE MARQUISE

MARQUISE — RAPAPORT: (4.00—4.99 CT.): 2/7/97

	IF	VVS1	VVS2	VS1	VS2	SI1	SI2	SI3	I1	I2	I3
D	315	229	199	179	159	132	95	85	73	40	21
E	229	199	179	159	142	125	90	80	68	37	20
F	199	179	159	142	129	115	86	76	64	35	19
G	179	159	140	129	115	100	82	71	60	33	18
H	154	140	125	115	100	90	75	66	56	31	17
I	120	110	105	100	90	80	65	57	48	29	16
J	91	86	81	76	71	65	55	49	42	27	15
K	74	70	66	63	59	55	50	44	38	24	15
L	59	57	55	52	50	45	42	37	31	22	14
M	46	44	42	40	38	35	30	27	25	20	12

MARQUISE — RAPAPORT: (5.00—5.99 CT.): 2/7/97

	IF	VVS1	VVS2	VS1	VS2	SI1	SI2	SI3	I1	I2	I3
D	445	310	280	250	225	185	125	105	80	44	24
E	309	280	250	225	203	170	120	100	75	42	22
F	279	250	225	203	176	150	115	95	72	40	20
G	249	225	200	176	155	135	110	90	68	38	19
H	215	195	170	155	135	115	95	80	62	36	18
I	157	147	142	130	115	95	80	70	57	34	17
J	115	110	105	100	90	80	70	62	52	31	16
K	92	88	85	80	75	70	60	54	47	28	16
L	71	69	68	66	62	57	48	46	42	25	15
M	51	49	47	45	42	38	34	30	22	13	

MARQUISE MARQUISE MARQUISE MARQUISE MARQUISE MARQUISE MARQUISE MARQUISE MARQUISE MARQUISE MARQUISE

RAPAPORT DIAMOND REPORT

Tel: 212-354-0575 ✦ Fax: 212-840-0243 ✦ 15 West 47th Street, New York, NY 10036 ✦ Internet: www.diamonds.net
February 7, 1997 Volume 20 No. 6: APPROXIMATE HIGH CASH ASKING PRICE INDICATIONS Page 39

EMERALD CUTS SPOT CASH N.Y.-FINE CUT, in Hundreds US$ Per Carat

The *Rapaport Diamond Report* is pleased to announce that we have begun publishing monthly prices for Marquise and Emerald Cut diamonds. Trade discounts for these price sheets are similar to the discounts for the round price sheet.

APPROXIMATE CONVERSION SCALE FOR OTHER SHAPES:

Radiant: As Emerald Cut prices with possibility of 1% to 3% premiums for scarce items.
Princess: Strong demand. 3% to 5% premiums over Emerald Cut prices.

Notice: Fancy shape diamonds are more complex than round diamonds and much harder to valuate. The quality of cut, proportions, and the overall shape of the fancy shape diamond all have a great impact on price and liquidity. Poorly cut stones may trade at substantial discounts, while well-shaped fine cut stones may trade at a premium. There is also a higher degree of availability difficulties in the fancy market and you may have to pay significantly higher prices for a select fine stone. Matching stones may also require a premium. It is not advisable to trade diamonds solely on the basis of the grading report. All stones should be examined by an expert. Consumers are cautioned to consult with a reputable jeweler to avoid buying a poorly cut, treated or misrepresented diamond. These price indications should only be used as a general guideline. Prices vary. This price sheet is not an offering to sell.

Prices for fine cut stones only. Medium and poorly cut stones may trade at very large discounts.
Large 6 ct+ D–G SI+ Emerald Cuts bringing better prices than Pear Shapes.

RAPAPORT: (.18—.22 CT.): 2/7/97   EMERALDS   RAPAPORT: (.23—.29 CT.): 2/7/97

	IF-VVS	VS	SI1	SI2	SI3	I1	I2	I3	IF-VVS	VS	SI1	SI2	SI3	I1	I2	I3
D–F	11.4	9.5	8.6	7.6	7.1	6.4	5.2	3.8	14.3	12.4	9.5	8.6	7.6	6.9	5.7	4.3
G–H	9.5	8.6	7.6	7.1	6.7	6.1	4.9	3.3	12.4	10.0	8.6	7.6	7.1	6.7	5.2	3.8
I–J	8.4	7.6	7.1	6.7	6.2	5.7	4.6	2.9	10.0	9.0	7.9	7.1	6.8	6.4	4.8	3.3
K–L	7.1	6.7	6.2	5.5	5.2	4.8	3.8	2.5	8.6	8.1	7.1	6.3	6.0	5.7	4.3	2.9
M–N	6.3	5.2	4.8	4.3	4.0	3.7	3.2	2.1	7.1	6.2	5.2	4.8	4.4	4.0	3.5	2.5

EMERALDS EMERALDS EMERALDS EMERALDS EMERALDS EMERALDS EMERALDS EMERALDS EMERALDS EMERALDS
EMERALD CUTS : EMERALD CUTS : EMERALD CUTS : EMERALD CUTS : EMERALD CUTS : EMERALD CUTS : EMERALD CUTS

RAPAPORT: (.30—.37 CT.): 2/7/97   EMERALDS   RAPAPORT: (.38—.45 CT.) 2/7/97

	IF	VVS1	VVS2	VS1	VS2	SI1	SI2	SI3	I1	I2	I3	IF	VVS1	VVS2	VS1	VS2	SI1	SI2	SI3	I1	I2	I3
D	30	28	26	25	21	19	16	14	12	9	7	33	31	30	28	24	21	19	16	13	10	9
E	28	26	24	21	19	18	15	14	11	8	6	31	30	28	26	23	20	18	15	12	9	8
F	26	24	22	19	18	17	14	13	10	7	6	29	28	25	24	22	19	17	14	11	8	7
G	24	22	20	18	17	16	14	13	9	7	5	27	25	23	22	20	18	16	13	10	8	7
H	20	19	18	17	16	15	13	12	8	6	5	24	23	21	20	19	17	15	12	9	7	6
I	16	15	15	14	14	13	12	11	8	6	4	20	19	18	17	15	14	13	11	8	7	6
J	15	14	14	13	12	11	10	9	7	5	4	17	16	16	15	14	13	11	9	7	6	5
K	13	12	11	11	10	10	9	8	7	5	4	16	15	14	13	12	11	10	8	7	6	5
L	11	10	10	9	9	8	8	7	5	4	3	13	12	12	11	10	9	8	7	6	5	4
M	10	9	9	8	8	7	7	6	5	3	3	11	11	10	10	9	8	6	6	5	4	4

EMERALDS EMERALDS EMERALDS EMERALDS EMERALDS EMERALDS EMERALDS EMERALDS EMERALDS EMERALDS

RAPAPORT: (.46—.49 CT.): 2/7/97   EMERALDS   RAPAPORT: (.50—.69 CT.): 2/7/97

	IF	VVS1	VVS2	VS1	VS2	SI1	SI2	SI3	I1	I2	I3	IF	VVS1	VVS2	VS1	VS2	SI1	SI2	SI3	I1	I2	I3
D	37	33	32	30	28	24	21	18	15	12	10	50	44	41	36	32	28	24	21	18	14	11
E	33	32	30	29	27	23	20	17	15	12	9	44	41	36	32	29	27	23	20	17	13	10
F	31	30	28	27	26	22	19	17	14	11	9	40	36	32	29	28	26	22	19	16	12	10
G	29	28	27	26	24	21	18	16	14	11	8	35	32	29	28	26	24	21	18	15	12	9
H	26	25	24	23	21	19	17	15	13	10	8	31	29	27	26	24	22	20	17	14	11	9
I	22	22	21	20	19	17	15	14	12	10	7	28	25	24	23	22	21	19	16	14	10	8
J	20	19	18	17	16	15	13	12	11	9	7	23	22	21	20	19	18	16	14	13	9	8
K	17	16	15	14	13	12	11	10	9	8	6	18	17	17	16	16	15	14	13	11	9	7
L	14	13	12	11	11	10	10	9	8	7	6	15	14	14	13	13	12	11	10	9	8	7
M	12	12	12	11	11	10	9	8	7	6	5	13	13	13	12	12	11	10	9	8	7	6

EMERALDS EMERALDS EMERALDS EMERALDS EMERALDS EMERALDS EMERALDS EMERALDS EMERALDS EMERALDS

RAPAPORT DIAMOND REPORT

Tel: 212-354-0575 ✦ Fax: 212-840-0243 ✦ 15 West 47th Street, New York, NY 10036 ✦ Internet: www.diamonds.net
February 7, 1997 Volume 20 No. 6: APPROXIMATE HIGH CASH ASKING PRICE INDICATIONS Page 40

SPOT CASH N.Y.: Emerald Shape Diamonds in Hundreds US$ Per Carat: THIS IS NOT AN OFFERING TO SELL
We grade SI-3 as a split SI2/I1 clarity. Price changes are in **Bold**. Price decreases are *italicized*.
Prices for fancy shapes are highly dependent on the cut. Poorly made stones often trade at huge
discounts while well-made stones may be hard to locate and bring premium prices.

RAPAPORT: (.70—.89 CT.): 2/7/97 — EMERALDS — RAPAPORT: (.90—.99 CT.): 2/7/97

	IF	VVS1	VVS2	VS1	VS2	SI1	SI2	SI3	I1	I2	I3	IF	VVS1	VVS2	VS1	VS2	SI1	SI2	SI3	I1	I2	I3
D	67	53	50	47	43	39	33	27	22	15	11	75	58	55	52	48	42	36	31	24	18	12
E	53	50	47	45	42	38	32	26	21	15	11	57	55	51	49	45	41	35	30	23	18	12
F	49	46	44	43	41	37	31	25	20	14	10	54	51	48	46	43	40	34	29	23	17	11
G	45	44	42	41	40	35	30	24	19	14	10	49	47	45	44	41	38	33	28	23	16	11
H	41	40	39	38	37	33	28	23	18	14	9	46	44	42	41	40	36	31	26	22	16	10
I	36	35	34	33	33	30	24	21	17	13	9	41	40	38	36	34	32	28	24	21	15	10
J	32	31	30	29	28	25	22	18	15	12	8	35	34	33	33	31	28	25	22	19	14	9
K	27	26	25	24	23	21	19	17	14	11	8	30	29	28	27	26	24	22	20	17	12	9
L	22	21	20	19	18	17	16	14	11	10	7	24	23	22	21	20	19	18	16	13	10	8
M	16	16	16	15	15	14	13	12	9	8	6	18	18	17	17	16	16	15	14	10	9	7
EMERALDS	EMERALDS		EMERALDS		EMERALDS		EMERALDS		EMERALDS		EMERALDS		EMERALDS		EMERALDS		EMERALDS		EMERALDS		EMERALDS

RAPAPORT: (1.00—1.49 CT.): 2/7/97 — EMERALDS — RAPAPORT: (1.50—1.99 CT.): 2/7/97

	IF	VVS1	VVS2	VS1	VS2	SI1	SI2	SI3	I1	I2	I3	IF	VVS1	VVS2	VS1	VS2	SI1	SI2	SI3	I1	I2	I3
D	111	73	64	62	58	49	42	35	28	21	12	127	82	73	70	66	58	48	40	32	23	13
E	72	64	61	59	56	47	41	34	27	20	12	81	73	69	66	64	56	47	39	31	22	13
F	63	60	58	56	53	45	40	33	26	20	11	72	70	67	64	60	54	46	38	30	21	12
G	58	57	54	53	50	43	38	32	25	19	11	67	65	62	59	55	50	44	37	29	20	12
H	55	52	50	48	45	40	36	30	24	18	10	59	58	56	53	50	45	40	35	28	19	11
I	47	46	44	42	40	37	32	28	23	17	10	51	50	48	45	43	40	36	32	26	18	11
J	41	39	37	35	33	31	28	24	21	14	10	46	45	43	41	39	35	32	27	23	16	10
K	35	34	33	32	30	29	26	22	20	13	10	39	38	37	35	33	31	29	25	22	15	10
L	30	29	28	27	25	23	21	18	16	11	9	32	31	30	29	28	26	23	20	18	15	10
M	25	24	23	22	21	19	17	16	13	11	7	27	26	25	24	23	21	19	18	15	13	8
EMERALDS	EMERALDS		EMERALDS		EMERALDS		EMERALDS		EMERALDS		EMERALDS		EMERALDS		EMERALDS		EMERALDS		EMERALDS		EMERALDS

EMERALD CUTS : EMERALD CUTS : EMERALD CUTS : EMERALD CUTS : EMERALD CUTS : EMERALD CUTS : EMERALD CUTS

*It is illegal and unethical to reproduce this price sheet. Please do not make copies.©1997

RAPAPORT: (2.00—2.99 CT.): 2/7/97 — EMERALDS — RAPAPORT: (3.00—3.99 CT.): 2/7/97

	IF	VVS1	VVS2	VS1	VS2	SI1	SI2	SI3	I1	I2	I3	IF	VVS1	VVS2	VS1	VS2	SI1	SI2	SI3	I1	I2	I3
D	200	127	114	104	95	73	55	45	37	23	14	280	190	166	151	132	112	78	70	60	32	18
E	125	114	102	97	85	70	53	43	35	23	14	190	166	148	132	121	105	74	65	56	30	17
F	112	102	95	85	78	66	52	42	33	22	14	162	148	130	121	112	97	70	61	52	28	16
G	99	95	83	78	72	61	49	39	32	21	13	144	130	118	112	98	85	67	58	50	26	15
H	92	82	73	69	61	53	45	37	30	20	12	125	117	104	98	85	71	64	54	45	24	14
I	71	68	63	57	50	46	40	34	27	19	12	102	95	90	83	69	63	54	47	41	23	14
J	57	54	51	48	43	40	34	30	25	18	11	77	73	68	64	59	52	45	39	33	21	13
K	46	43	41	40	37	34	31	26	23	17	11	62	59	56	51	49	44	38	34	30	19	12
L	37	35	33	32	29	27	25	22	19	15	10	49	47	44	41	40	35	32	28	24	17	11
M	30	29	27	26	24	23	21	19	16	14	8	35	33	32	31	29	26	23	22	20	16	9
EMERALDS	EMERALDS		EMERALDS		EMERALDS		EMERALDS		EMERALDS		EMERALDS		EMERALDS		EMERALDS		EMERALDS		EMERALDS		EMERALDS

RAPAPORT: (4.00—4.99 CT.): 2/7/97 — EMERALDS — RAPAPORT: (5.00—5.99 CT.): 2/7/97

	IF	VVS1	VVS2	VS1	VS2	SI1	SI2	SI3	I1	I2	I3	IF	VVS1	VVS2	VS1	VS2	SI1	SI2	SI3	I1	I2	I3
D	300	205	179	165	146	121	87	77	66	36	19	445	275	250	230	207	170	115	94	72	40	22
E	205	179	161	146	131	115	83	72	61	33	18	275	250	225	207	187	156	110	90	68	38	20
F	175	161	143	131	119	106	79	68	58	32	17	250	225	203	187	162	138	106	86	65	36	18
G	158	143	126	119	106	92	75	64	54	30	16	220	203	180	162	143	124	101	81	61	34	17
H	136	126	113	106	92	83	69	59	50	28	15	190	176	153	143	124	106	87	72	56	32	16
I	107	99	95	90	81	72	59	51	43	26	14	140	132	128	117	104	86	72	63	51	31	15
J	82	77	73	68	64	59	50	44	38	24	14	104	99	95	90	81	72	63	56	47	28	14
K	67	63	59	57	53	50	45	40	34	22	13	83	79	77	72	68	63	54	49	42	25	14
L	53	51	50	47	45	41	34	31	28	20	12	64	62	61	59	56	51	43	41	38	23	13
M	41	40	38	36	34	32	27	24	23	18	10	48	46	44	42	39	37	34	31	27	20	12
EMERALDS	EMERALDS		EMERALDS		EMERALDS		EMERALDS		EMERALDS		EMERALDS		EMERALDS		EMERALDS		EMERALDS		EMERALDS		EMERALDS

The report has two separate sections. The first section lists round, brilliant-cut diamonds from one point (.01 ct.) all the way up to five carats and ninety-nine points (5.99 ct.). This section of the list is very reliable because round, brilliant-cut stones are easier to grade than fancy-shape diamonds such as marquise or pear-shape diamonds. The reason for this is that rounds have much more uniformity in cutting standards than their fancy-shape counterparts. The assumption is that each of the round, brilliant diamonds listed is properly proportioned and that the cut or make is good. Rapaport uses the terms "RDC Spec A" and "RDC Spec B" to indicate good cutting proportions. If the cut is less than "RDC Spec A" then the per carat price of the diamond decreases. In some instances "excellent" and "ideal" cut stones bring substantially higher prices (10 to 15 percent) than well-cut stones ("RDC Spec A and B"). Poorly cut stones often trade at prices much lower (−10 to −40 percent) than well-cut stones.

The way the list works is that each box represents a range of sizes of a certain shape of diamond. Along the vertical axis the various color grades are specified and on the horizontal axis the various clarity grades are indicated. The shape of the diamond is indicated in the middle of the page.

Therefore, if you want to know the wholesale price of a round, brilliant-cut, one-carat diamond having the color grade of J and the clarity grade of SI1, simply look at the appropriate box (1.00–1.49 ct.). Follow the vertical column down until you find "J", then move across the page until you converge at the "SI1" column. The price at that intersection is 42. All prices on the Rapaport Diamond Report are quoted in hundreds of U.S. dollars per carat, so two zeros must be added to the numbers quoted. In this case 42 translates to $4,200 per carat. Therefore, the wholesale price of a well-proportioned, round, brilliant-cut, one-carat diamond having a color grade of "J" and a clarity grade of "SI1" during the month of January 1997 was $4,200 per carat.

RAPAPORT SPECIFICATIONS
FOR GIA GRADED ROUND DIAMONDS

RDC Spec	A	B
Depth %	57.5–62.5	57.0–63.0
Table %	55–64	55–65
Girdle	No extreme; no very thick	As "Spec A"
Culet	No large or chipped	As "Spec A"
Polish	"Good" or better	As "Spec A"
Symmetry	"Good" or better	As "Spec A"
Flourescence	No strong or medium	Medium OK but no Yellow
Comments	No Graining	Surface Graining OK
	No Crown Angle Comment	As "Spec A"
	No lasering	As "Spec A"
	No Color or Clarity Treatments	As "Spec A"

Stones that do not meet A or B are Rap Spec "C"

These specifications are subject to change without prior notice.

Rapaport Specifications for GIA Graded Round Diamonds.
Reprinted courtesy of Rapaport Diamond Report

The second part of the Rapaport Diamond Report deals with the wholesale New York cash asking prices for fancy-shape diamonds, including pear-shape, marquise, emerald-cut, radiant, princess, heart-shaped, and ovals. The prices for these shapes of diamonds are more problematic to determine because of the great variance in the way the stones are cut. Rapaport clearly states at the beginning of his fancy-shape report the following disclaimer:

The market for fancy shape diamonds is more complex than the rounds market and much harder to evaluate. The quality of cut, proportion, and overall shape of the fancy cut diamond all have great impact on price and liquidity. Poorly cut stones may trade at substantial

RAPAPORT: (1.00 − 1.49 CT.): 2/7/97

	IF	VVS1	VVS2	VS1	VS2	SI1	SI2	SI3	I1	I2	I3
D	164	111	96	78	68	60	54	43	35	24	15
E	111	98	79	72	66	59	53	42	34	24	14
F	97	80	72	69	64	58	51	41	33	23	14
G	79	72	68	65	61	56	49	39	32	22	13
H	69	66	63	60	57	53	47	38	31	21	13
I	61	58	55	53	50	47	42	37	30	19	12
J	54	52	50	48	46	(42)	38	33	28	18	12
K	49	47	46	44	41	39	35	31	26	17	11
L	43	42	40	38	36	34	31	28	23	16	10
M	35	34	33	31	29	27	25	23	19	15	10

W: 79.40 = 0.00%   ✧✧✧   T: 45.17 = 0.00%

*Rapaport Diamond Report. Reprinted courtesy of
Rapaport Diamond Report*

discounts, while well-shaped, fine cut stones may trade at a premium. There is also a higher degree of availability difficulties in the fancy market and you may have to pay significantly higher prices for a select fine stone. Matching stones may also require a premium. It is not advisable to trade diamonds solely on the basis of the grading report. All stones should be examined by an expert. Consumers are cautioned to consult with a reputable jeweler to avoid buying a poorly cut, treated, or misrepresented diamond. These price indications should only be used as a general guideline. Prices vary.

The Rapaport Diamond Report uses pear-shape diamonds as the standard. All the prices that are provided are for well-proportioned pear shapes. Once again, each box represents a range of sizes of pear-shape diamonds. Along the vertical axis the various color grades are specified and on the horizontal axis the various clarity grades are indicated. The shape of the diamond is indicated in the middle of the page.

Consequently, if you want to determine the wholesale price of a two-carat pear-shape diamond having the color grade of I and the clarity grade of VS2, simply look at the appropriate box (2.00–2.99 ct.). Follow the vertical column down until you find "I," then move across the page until you intersect at the "VS2" column. The price at that convergence is 59. Remember, all prices on the Rapaport Diamond Report are quoted in hundreds of U.S. dollars per carat, so two zeros must be added to the numbers quoted. In this case 59 translates to $5,900 per carat. Therefore, the wholesale price of a well-proportioned, two-carat pear-shaped diamond having a color grade of "I" and a clarity grade of "VS2" during the month of February 1997 was $5,900 per carat or $11,800 for the entire stone (2 carats multiplied by $5,900 per carat).

Let's assume you are interested in purchasing a well-made, two-carat, heart-shaped diamond having the color grade of I and the clarity grade of VS2. To determine the price, calculate the percentage change for this specific stone as indicated at the very start of the Fancy Shape report (on page 90). According to Rapaport's approximate conversion scale, the difference between an "I" color grade, "VS2" clarity grade, pear-shape two-carat diamond and a two-carat heart-shape diamond having identical color and clarity grades and cut is 0 to 5 percent discount for large sizes. Therefore the approximate high-end price of this stone per carat, assuming a 0 percent discount, would be $5,900 per carat or $11,800 for the entire stone (2 carats multiplied by $5,900 per carat). The low-end price would be $5,900 per carat less 5 percent, which would calculate to $5,605 per carat or $11,210 for the stone ($5,605 multiplied by 2.00 carats).

PEARS : PEARS : PEARS : PEARS : PEARS
RAPAPORT: (2.00 – 2.99 CT.): 2/7/97

	IF	VVS1	VVS2	VS1	VS2	SI1	SI2	SI3	I1	I2	I3
D	212	143	129	115	105	82	62	52	41	27	16
E	143	129	115	107	94	79	60	49	39	26	15
F	129	115	107	94	88	75	58	47	37	24	15
G	115	107	94	88	81	69	55	45	35	23	14
H	107	93	82	77	69	61	50	42	33	22	13
I	82	77	72	65	(59)	53	46	39	30	21	13
J	64	61	58	54	49	45	39	34	28	20	12
K	52	49	47	45	42	39	35	30	25	19	12
L	42	40	38	36	33	31	29	25	21	17	11
M	34	33	31	30	28	26	24	22	18	15	9

Rapaport Diamond Report. Reprinted courtesy of
Rapaport Diamond Report

It is possible to calculate the wholesale price of any radiant, princess, oval, or heart-shape diamond by using Rapaport's conversion table. By following the procedure of first finding the size and quality of a pear-shape diamond, which acts as a standard or base number, it is a matter of simple mathematics to determine the wholesale price of another fancy-shape stone. Once again, for example, suppose you were offered a poorly proportioned, GIA-certified emerald-cut diamond weighing 1.50 carats and having a color grade of G and a clarity grade of VS1. The retailer who offered this diamond is asking $6,000 per carat or $9,000 for the stone. Is this a good deal?

By using the Rapaport Diamond Report you would go to the section dealing with emerald cuts and look in the appropriate box (1.50–1.99 ct.) for price information on an emerald-cut diamond weighing 1.50 carats and having a color grade of G and a clarity grade of VS1. The price that is indicated is $5,900 per carat for a well-cut, good-proportioned stone.

I would calculate that the percentage discount for a poorly proportioned emerald-cut diamond weighing 1.50 carats is between 25 percent and 40 percent. (Discount percentages for badly proportioned diamonds are noted in the report, or you can call Rapaport at 212–354–0575 and ask specific questions.) Therefore the stone, depending on how poorly proportioned it is, has the value of $4,425 to $3,540 per carat. The most this entire diamond could be worth is $6,637.50 and the least would be $5,310. Therefore, the price of $9,000 that the retail jeweler asked for this stone is much too high.

The Rapaport Diamond Report is an extremely useful tool because it clearly eliminates the secrecy surrounding the whole-

EMERALDS EMERALDS EMERALDS EMERALDS
RAPAPORT: (1.50 – 1.99 CT.): 2/7/97

	IF	VVS1	VVS2	VS1	VS2	SI1	SI2	SI3	I1	I2	I3
D	127	82	73	70	66	58	48	40	32	23	13
E	81	73	69	66	64	56	47	39	31	22	13
F	72	70	67	64	60	54	46	38	30	21	12
G	67	65	62	(59)	55	50	44	37	29	20	12
H	59	58	56	53	50	45	40	35	28	19	11
I	51	50	48	45	43	40	36	32	26	18	11
J	46	45	43	41	39	35	32	27	23	16	10
K	39	38	37	35	33	31	29	25	22	15	10
L	32	31	30	29	28	26	23	20	18	13	10
M	27	26	25	24	23	21	19	18	15	13	8

EMERALDS EMERALDS EMERALDS EMERALDS

*Rapaport Diamond Report. Reprinted courtesy of
Rapaport Diamond Report*

sale price of diamonds. Now that you are aware of the existence of this remarkable report the next question is how the average consumer can use it to his or her advantage. The first major benefit of using the Rap-sheet is that consumers can determine what shapes, sizes, and qualities of diamonds are available within their budget. This will make the search for the best possible diamond easier.

Sometimes it is necessary or desirable to sell a diamond or a piece of diamond jewelry that was purchased at a wholesale price. It will be far less costly to sell that merchandise since the owner can determine the current wholesale worth of his or her merchandise by using a combination of the GIA Diamond Grading Report and the Rapaport Diamond Report. If the stone was purchased at wholesale it is possible for the owner to make a profit on the sale if wholesale prices have increased sufficiently. At the very worst, the loss will be minimized. If the owner purchased the merchandise on the retail level, similar to our example in the Introduction to this book, chances are he or she will lose a great deal of money regardless of the direction wholesale prices have taken.

When I first moved to Florida in 1980, I was employed by a prestigious Miami retailer as an estate buyer. My job involved buying jewelry from individuals who wanted to sell. The usual scenario was that an older, retired couple had one large diamond ring and two or three children. To avoid a family feud after the couple's death they decided to sell the diamond and divide the money equally among the children. The major problem was that the couple didn't have any idea what their jewelry was worth. The only thing they remembered was what they had paid for the piece thirty or forty years earlier. Naturally, with the passage of that much time and the normal rate of inflation, the merchandise had appreciated enormously. If this book had existed in 1980, they might have known to first send their diamond to the Gemological Institute of America for a Diamond Grading

Report and then use the Rapaport Diamond Report to determine what their diamond was really worth. Unfortunately for most of these sellers, they sold their merchandise far beneath the current wholesale prices, usually losing thousands of dollars.

My suggestion would be to purchase diamonds or diamond jewelry only from a business that allows knowledgeable consumers to look at the Rap-sheet and work from it. I would not deal with any company that does not subscribe to the Rapaport Diamond Report and make it available to consumers upon request. Only by insisting upon purchasing a diamond with a corresponding GIA Diamond Grading Report and working off the Rapaport Diamond Report can the consumer be certain that he or she will make a prudent purchase. It is not unreasonable to allow a retailer or dealer to make a profit on any transaction. If you can negotiate a price anywhere from 10 to 20 percent above the Rapaport Diamond Report, generally you have made a good deal.

Unfortunately, the Rapaport Diamond Report is strictly a wholesale diamond price list meant to be seen and used only by members of the jewelry trade. Rapaport will only sell his list to those who can prove that they are active retail jewelers, jewelry manufacturers, or jewelry wholesalers. If you do not work in the jewelry industry you can not buy a Rapaport Diamond Report directly.

However, I have developed a list that you may purchase that closely follows the New York wholesale asking prices for diamonds. My list is updated each month and will furnish you with the pricing information you require to make an informed diamond(s) purchase. The list may be obtained by sending a check or money order for $9.95 and a stamped self-addressed envelope to:

FJA, Inc.
650 NE 126th Street
Miami, Florida 33161

CHAPTER 10

The Power of Fallacious Advertising

I think we are all familiar with the promotional advertisements that proclaim "A Diamond Is Forever." Usually the scene has a couple, the man in a dark tuxedo and the woman in a lovely gown, staring longingly into each other's eyes. A deep, sophisticated voice says something like, "Show her you truly love her. Give her a diamond. A diamond is forever."

These highly successful, worldwide advertising campaigns are sponsored and paid for by De Beers Limited, the international diamond syndicate based in London, England, that controls approximately 80 percent of the world's rough or uncut diamonds. Their gross yearly international sales of unpolished diamonds exceeds four billion U.S. dollars. They have spent hundreds of millions of dollars on advertisements that have promoted diamond jewelry sales in every major industrialized country and the results are incredible. For example, diamonds are by far the most popular gemstone in the United States and Canada. According to the Rapaport Diamond Report, diamonds and diamond jewelry combined accounted for 38.9 percent of all North American jewelry sales, making them the strongest category. Prior to World War II diamond engagement rings were unknown in Japan. Today, as a result of massive advertising by De Beers, more than 94 percent of Japanese women and 87 percent of the men in engaged couples are convinced that an engagement ring should have a diamond worth three months of the groom's salary. Astonishing as these phenomenal sales results are, I often wonder what exactly the phrase "A diamond is forever" really means.

The alluring advertising by De Beers is really meaningless compared to the ambiguous, deceptive, and fraudulent advertisements we are about to scrutinize. The examples that I am going to use are actual advertisements that have been published in large metropolitan newspapers. The reason I am criticizing these

Diamond Advertisement

advertisements is not to embarrass or harass the advertisers, but to help you understand how to read and interpret them.

In our first example we have a catalog page that is promoting diamond stud earrings, solitaire diamond engagement rings, and diamond pendants. Notice that we have two engagement rings that have a one-carat solitaire center stone. One ring is advertised for $2,895 (top, right-hand column) and the other is advertised for $1,989 (top, center column). I cannot tell from the information provided why there is a difference in price of $906. The only clue I have is that the more expensive ring is advertised as "Prestige Quality." My question is, what does "prestige quality" mean? We know that the GIA diamond grading system doesn't have any such designation. I cannot compare the quality of these two stones from the advertisement because I do not know the actual carat weight, color grade, or clarity grade of either stone. Furthermore, I do not have a clue as to the quality of the "make" or proportions of either stone. In short, I do not know anything about these stones except that they are being advertised and the price the retailer is asking. The same is true for every other diamond advertised on this page. You, the consumer, are not given any useful information whatsoever, and it gets worse. Do you see any mention of a GIA Diamond Grading Report accompanying any of the diamonds being advertised? You do not because this company does not want you to have any factual information which will enable you to determine precisely how much profit they are trying to make on their diamonds.

There are other important questions that this advertisement does not answer. For example, are the diamonds used in the pairs of stud earrings advertised well matched? Do they have the same diameter, are they the same body color, are they equal in weight, and do they have the same size tables? What is the per carat price of each stone?

This advertisement assumes you know absolutely nothing about diamonds and jewelry. They are treating you like an igno-

Diamond Advertisement

rant consumer and we all know what happens to uneducated buyers in this society. When you see ads like this in your local newspaper ask yourself whether or not you feel like dealing with companies that are trying to take advantage of you.

In our second example we have an advertisement for a diamond tennis bracelet with a total carat weight (T.W.) of 7 carats. My first question is, how many stones does this bracelet have? And what is the weight of each individual diamond? The way this advertisement is written you do not have any idea what size diamonds are being used. Are the diamonds uniform in size or are they graduated (from smaller to larger sizes)? In addition, the color or clarity grade of the diamonds is not specified, nor is the quality of the make or proportions of the stones disclosed. There is no mention of a GIA Diamond Grading Report or any other type of appraisal that accompanies this bracelet. The advertisement states that you can save $2,500 but gives no further explanation. How can you save $2,500? Is the real price of the bracelet $4,495 ($1,995 + $2,500), and how did the

Diamond Advertisement

company come to that figure, or is this just another case of the deceptive and fraudulent jewelry advertisement that runs so rampant through the media? As a last point, which will be closely examined in the jewelry section of this book, this company does not even disclose whether the actual tennis bracelet is gold. If it is made of gold they do not mention the karat of the gold (10, 14, or 18 karat) or the length or weight of the bracelet. In short, once again, very little useful or analytical information is given. Consequently, there is no possibility of making an intelligent decision as to the intrinsic value of the merchandise.

The last example has to do with the announcement of a "big" sale on jewelry and the amount of discount offered. I am always amazed when I see a large department store offer 60 percent off plus another 20 percent off on selected items. The question you have to ask yourself is, how much did they mark these items up in the first place? Stores are not in business to lose money and these giant newspaper advertisements are not cheap. So how is it possible that every week one store or another offers you such gigantic discounts? The only reasonable explanation I can come up with is that they have marked up the items 300 percent or 400 percent and can easily afford to give away large discounts and still make money.

Therefore, do not be fooled by exaggerated sales, unrealistic discounts, and bargains that sound too good to be true. Do not be taken in by the deceptive and fraudulent advertising practices that retailers use to try to separate you from your hard-earned cash. Ask relevant questions and demand disclosure of all pertinent information regarding carat weight, clarity, color, and the make of the diamond(s) you are considering purchasing so that you will be able to make an informed and intelligent decision. Never rely on the quality assigned by the seller of diamonds but only on a GIA-graded diamond report or the opinion of a neutral, qualified gemologist-appraiser.

CHAPTER 11

How to Find an Expert You Can Trust

A woman wanted to buy a two-carat diamond for herself. After a few months of searching she found a stone that she really liked. The price seemed reasonable and the diamond came with a recent (within six months) GIA Diamond Grading Report. She made an arrangement with the seller to have the stone independently appraised; if the evaluation was good she would purchase it. She then took the stone to a jeweler who was a certified gemologist and told him she wanted to purchase a diamond the exact same size and quality as the one she had in order to make a pair of earrings. The jeweler carefully examined the woman's stone and after a few moments gave her a price. The woman asked the gemologist some questions pertaining to the characteristics of the stone she had, including the weight of the stone, the diameter and depth of the stone, and lastly the color and clarity grades. She wrote down the particulars and thanked the jeweler for his help. She then compared the gemologist's conclusions to the GIA Diamond Grading Report and the results matched. Being very cautious, this woman repeated the procedure two more times at different jewelers. The results all matched and the retail prices were significantly higher than the price she was paying, so she was nearly satisfied. The last thing she did was to call the Gemological Institute of America and verify that the Diamond Grading Report was not a forgery.

In another instance a man wanted to purchase a one-carat diamond for his wife. He found a stone he liked that included a

GIA Diamond Grading Report. Not knowing if the diamond corresponded with the report, he asked the owner for a photocopy of the certificate. He took the photocopy to a gemologist who owned a retail store and showed him the copy of the report. He told him that he owned the stone and would like to sell it. The gemologist said he would be interested in buying it. They made an appointment for the following day.

The next day the man went to the seller of the diamond and told him he wanted to get an independent appraisal of the diamond. As security the man paid the selling price of the diamond in cash with the understanding that he could have his money back if the appraisal was not satisfactory.

The man went back to the gemologist and showed him the diamond. The gemologist very carefully examined and measured the diamond. After about ten minutes the gemologist made the man an offer. The man replied that the offer was a little low for the quality stated on the report. The gemologist gave some explanation for his offer, but he did not argue about the report. At this point the man knew the GIA Diamond Grading Report corresponded with the diamond.

I do not approve or endorse the methods used by the man or woman to verify the diamonds they wanted to purchase. I know when purchasing diamonds or jewelry that there are any number of instances where you need the opinion of a certified expert in order to make an informed and confident decision. When those occasions arise I believe you should hire a qualified, impartial, certified expert and pay that person a reasonable fee for his or her services.

There are a number of situations where the opinion of a qualified gemologist or appraiser is required in order to make an intelligent decision when purchasing diamonds or fine jewelry. In the following paragraphs I will give you some of the instances in which I firmly believe you should consult with an expert:

1. IF YOU ARE BUYING A DIAMOND A HALF-CARAT IN SIZE OR LARGER THAT INCLUDES A GIA DIAMOND REPORT.

You need to confirm that the report is not a forgery and that it describes accurately the diamond you are considering purchasing. You should also have the cut or make of the diamond evaluated and documented. This will supplement the shortcomings of the GIA Diamond Grading Report (see Chapter 8);

2. IF YOU ARE BUYING A DIAMOND LESS THAN A HALF-CARAT IN SIZE THAT DOES NOT COME WITH A GIA DIAMOND GRADING REPORT.

If you are interested in knowing what you are purchasing with regard to the accuracy of the carat weight, and the quality of the color, clarity, and cut of the diamond, it is necessary to consult with an expert. After the characteristics of the diamond have been determined you can calculate what the wholesale price of the stone should be by consulting the Rapaport Diamond Report;

3. IF YOU ARE BUYING DIAMOND JEWELRY SUCH AS A RING, BRACELET, OR PENDANT THAT IS COMPRISED OF A NUMBER OF SMALL STONES.

For example, you want to purchase a diamond tennis bracelet that contains thirty diamonds with a total carat weight of 6.00 carats. Each stone weighs approximately twenty points or one-fifth of a carat (6.00 divided by 30 equals .20 carat). This type of merchandise, with a number of small stones, does not come with a GIA Diamond Grading Report. The only way you can determine the actual quality of the diamonds and consequently the wholesale price is by obtaining the expert opinion of an independent, impartial certified gemologist-appraiser;

4. If You Are Purchasing a Number of Small, Polished, Loose Diamonds to Be Used in Jewelry.

For example, you want to buy forty diamonds that are uniform in size and have a total carat weight of two carats to be used in a ring. These diamonds weigh .05 carat (five points or one-twentieth of a carat) each (2.00 carats divided by 40 stones equal .05 carat). These stones are too small and too numerous to warrant the expense of a GIA analysis. Therefore, the only way you can determine the uniformity, quality, and wholesale price of the stones is to obtain the opinion of an expert;

5. If You Are Interested in Purchasing a Bracelet or a Neck Chain That Is Represented As 18 Karat Gold.

How do you know that the piece is really 18 karat, or even gold, for that matter? Once again, to make an informed decision, you need the opinion of an expert.

The first step in recognizing a certified expert in the jewelry field is to check their educational credentials. In the United States and Canada there are two diplomas that are widely recognized as fine gemological degrees. The highest degree from the Gemological Institute of America is GG (Graduate Gemologist) and the Gemological Association of Great Britain awards an FGA (Fellow of the Gemological Association) in the United States and FCGA (Fellow of the Canadian Gemological Association) in Canada. I would only employ a gemologist who had earned one of these diplomas.

In addition, the gemologist-appraiser should belong to a professional society such as the American Gem Society, which bestows the title of "Certified Gemologist Appraiser," or the International Society of Appraisers, which awards the title of "Certified Appraiser of Personal Property" to their members.

A good place to find the names of qualified gemologist-appraisers is the classified business section of the telephone directory (Yellow Pages) under the heading of *appraisers* or *jewelry*. If you are unsuccessful at locating a qualified gemologist-appraiser you can call any of the following organizations for the name of their member(s) nearest to your home or place of employment:

The American Gem Society
8881 W. Sahara Avenue
Las Vegas, Nevada 89117-5865
Telephone: (702) 255-6500
Fax: (702) 255-7420

Request the names and addresses of Certified Gemologist Appraisers in your area.

The International Society of Appraisers
16040 Christensen Road, Suite 320
Seattle, Washington 98188-2929
Telephone: (206) 241-0359
Fax: (206) 241-0436

Request the names and addresses of Certified Appraisers of Personal Property in your area.

The National Association of Jewelry Appraisers
P.O. Box 6558
Annapolis, Maryland 21401-0558
Telephone: (301) 261-8270

Request the names and addresses of National Jewelry Appraisers in your area.

I would make certain that the certified gemologist-appraiser you employ has at least two years of practical experience. Formal education is an excellent place to start, but it takes time to view thousands of diamonds and become an expert diamond grader. It is also necessary to work in the field to become thoroughly familiar with trade practices. The easiest way to determine how much experience a gemologist-appraiser has is to ask him how long he has been involved in the business. If he says less than two years, thank him for his time but walk away.

An appraiser's fee should be based upon the amount of time he spends on your report. He should inform you at the beginning how much he intends to charge per hour for his services. He should also indicate, based on his experience, how much time the appraisal should take. It is unethical and a conflict of interest for a certified appraiser to base his fee on a percentage of the total value of the item(s) he is evaluating. For example, if an appraiser charges you 1 percent of the value of the diamond you have brought him for an evaluation, what is to prevent him from giving you an unrealistically high value for that stone? Remember, the higher the value he places on your diamond, the higher the fee the appraiser is entitled to charge. That is why you should never agree to an appraisal fee based on a percentage of value.

Once you have hired a certified appraiser, it is also unethical of him to downgrade your merchandise for the purpose of selling you his own goods. If an appraiser tries to turn the appraisal into a situation in which he attempts to sell you his own merchandise he is behaving in a highly unprofessional manner. Under these circumstances I would immediately inform the appraiser that you are not interested in his selection of merchandise and would like to have the item you brought honestly evaluated.

A certified appraiser should be able to determine the value of an item(s) on the retail or wholesale level. Depending upon your purpose for having the valuation performed, you may request either the retail or wholesale price(s) or both. The retail price is usually called the retail replacement cost and the wholesale price may be called the fair market value. If you have requested the wholesale price on a diamond or fine jewelry you should request the latest Rapaport Diamond Report from the appraiser only after he has finished his report. If there is a price discrepancy between the appraiser's wholesale price and Rapaport's price for your quality stone you should inquire why the difference exists.

It should not be necessary for you to leave your merchandise with an appraiser. Once you have decided to hire an appraiser, make an appointment to bring in your item(s). The appraiser should utilize the appointment time to carefully examine the jewelry and make notes. When the appraiser is finished analyzing the items take them back. During the examination make sure that you and your goods are not separated, especially if a diamond must be unmounted from a ring. The appraiser may not give you his written report immediately, but he will have all the information required to do the report from his notes. My advice is, don't leave your valuable merchandise with anyone!

CHAPTER 12

The Payoff

By this time you probably know which diamond you want to buy. You know how much money you're willing to spend on a stone. You should have referred to the Rapaport Diamond Report to determine what the current wholesale New York asking prices for diamonds are. You have browsed at various retail stores and decided on the shape, size, and quality of the diamond(s) you prefer. The only question remaining is where to purchase the diamond.

The first place you might want to try is your local independent jeweler. Using the business telephone directory I would look for a retail jeweler who advertises that he is a GIA Graduate Gemologist who specializes in diamond sales. It is also important that the store be successfully established for at least five years. This helps ensure that this is an ongoing business that, hopefully, will be there if you require their services in the future. I would avoid regional or national chains because they typically do not have the flexibility in their pricing policy that an independent jeweler has, unless they advertise that they sell their diamonds off the Rapaport list.

Having made your selection of merchants, you should use the direct approach. Introduce yourself to the owner or manager and tell him that you want to purchase a certain size diamond, of a specific shape and quality. Tell him that the stone must be accompanied by a GIA Diamond Grading Report and that you want to establish the price of the diamond from the most current Rapaport Diamond Report. It might also be a good idea to take this book with you to the store because that will signal to the jeweler that you have done your homework and that you know how to purchase a diamond intelligently.

If the retailer is unwilling to show you the most recent Rap-sheet or establish a price from it, thank the merchant for his time and leave. You definitely do not want to buy from a retailer who is averse to disclosing the information you need.

One of the best sources to purchase from are diamond dealers. These merchants either cut and polish rough diamonds themselves, import polished stones from overseas, or do a combination of both activities. They normally sell their stones to other diamond merchants, jewelry manufacturers, or retail jewelry stores. They can be found in the business telephone directory of large metropolitan areas such as New York, Chicago, Miami, and Los Angeles under the classification of *diamonds—wholesale* or *diamond cutters*.

The best way to approach these companies is to call them and tell them you wish to purchase a diamond of a specific size and quality and pay for it immediately. Some dealers will tell you that they only sell to wholesalers. Your response should be, "Do they pay you immediately, as I am offering to do?" If you are persistent, and take the time to make a few telephone calls, you will find a dealer who will sell you a diamond.

Another approach that works well is to send letters to a number of different diamond dealers explaining that you are in the market to buy a specific diamond. The following correspondence is a good example of the type of letter that elicits a positive response.

The reason diamond merchants will react to this letter is that they are always looking for sales. Their business is dependent on selling stones and getting paid for the diamonds as quickly as possible. When they sell their diamonds *in the trade* (to other jewelers) they have to extend credit for sixty, ninety, and sometimes one hundred and twenty days before they get

Mildred Newhouser
1275 Rose Boulevard
Sea Cliff, ME 04101

December 15th, 1997

Sunburst Diamond Company
2300 Commerce Boulevard
New York, NY 10061

Dear Sir,
    I would like to purchase a well-proportioned, 1.50
carat, round, brilliant-cut diamond having a color grade
of K and a clarity grade of SI2. This stone must be
certified by a recent GIA Diamond Grading Certificate.
I am willing to use the most recent Rapaport list to
determine the price of this stone for which I am willing
to pay immediately. If you have a stone similar to the
one that I describe please contact me at (207) 555-9986.
    Thank you in advance for your time and help in this
matter.

Sincerely,

Mildred Newhouser

Mildred Newhouser

paid. This requirement to finance sales sometimes causes cash
flow problems for the merchant, including jeopardizing his
ability to pay his bills. Therefore, an offer to buy a significant-size

diamond at a fair price and get paid immediately is more tempta-
tion than most merchants can bear. Consequently, don't be surprised if your phone rings off the hook after you send out this
letter.

In my opinion, the best way to purchase a diamond is to buy
one through the Internet. There is a network, owned and oper-
ated by the Rapaport Diamond Report, whose Internet address is
http://www.diamonds.net, that is totally devoted to the jewelry
industry. This network will allow the public to contact a wide
assortment of diamond dealers-wholesalers, jewelry manufacturers, discount retailers, gemstone (colored stone) dealers, and
jewelry suppliers (finding houses) and purchase diamonds, gemstones, and fine jewelry at wholesale prices. The reason this is
possible is that the overhead expenses connected with electronic
distribution of goods and services is a fraction of the costs associated with the traditional methods of sales. I can very easily work
from my house or garage and set up my own website on this network, selling diamonds at wholesale prices to the public, and still
make an acceptable profit. In this arrangement everybody wins!
I, as a diamond dealer, do not have to depend on a retailer to sell
my merchandise. I do not have to extend credit and hope that I
will be paid sometime in the distant future. I do not have to
watch the price of my diamonds being marked up 100 percent or
more by a retailer, making those stones far more difficult to sell. I
can sell to the public for the same wholesale price as I would sell
to the retail jewelry store, make the same profit, and get paid
immediately. Given this logic, why wouldn't I want to develop
this type of business? Hundreds of prominent dealers are involved in electronic distribution, and that is why you are now
able to purchase diamonds at prices never before possible, as long
as you know what you are doing.

This network has a number of features that make it very easy
to use. On the bottom of the home page is an area labeled **Public
Discussion Forums** (you might have to scroll to it). If you are

interested in purchasing a diamond you access the *diamond portion* of the forums by clicking your mouse on that box. You may then list the type of stone you are looking for and either your e-mail address or your phone number. Diamond merchants are always surfing this forum (which is a combination of a bulletin board and a chat room) and they will certainly reply to your notice. A typical notice might look like this:

I want to purchase a 2.50-carat round, brilliant-cut diamond that is well proportioned, having the color grade of L and the clarity grade of I1. The stone must be accompanied by a recent (less than six months old) corresponding GIA Diamond Grading Report. I am willing to purchase this stone off the most recent Rapaport Diamond Report. Please reply to Farower@aol.com or (305) 891-0000.

Another fantastic feature of this network is a section called **Jewelry Related Websites**. This is where various jewelry related companies interested in doing business with the public advertise. They have developed their own websites that are linked to this network and may be accessed through this area. You can go to specialized areas that are dedicated to diamond dealers-wholesalers, jewelry manufacturers, retailers, and jewelry suppliers. If, for example, you are interested in purchasing a diamond, you can access any of the many diamond merchants and find out what they have to offer. You can also request information or ask them questions by using their e-mail addresses. In short, this section allows you to access companies throughout the world and purchase diamonds and fine jewelry directly at wholesale prices.

Another excellent feature of this network is the *Jewelry Trade Directory*. As the name implies, most of the companies that are willing to do business through the network are listed in this guide in alphabetical order. You can scan through this list if you are searching for a certain type of company or a certain geographical location, or you can go directly to the firm on which you would like information by using the *Jewelry Trade Directory Search Forum*.

There is another network devoted strictly to the jewelry industry that you should also look at. It is called the polygon network and the address is **http://www.polygon.net**. This network offers many of the same features as www.diamonds.net, but it is an alternative resource that might provide additional useful information and sources.

At this point you should be aware of how to choose a diamond(s) based on your budget, personal preferences, and inside trade information relating to a diamond's carat, color, clarity, and cut. You also know where and how to shop for the best prices based on the Rapaport Diamond Report and how to find and utilize a gemologist-appraiser to validate the quality and size of diamond you are purchasing and to confirm that the GIA Diamond Grading Report corresponds to the stone you are purchasing.

CHAPTER 13

Insurance Appraisals

A few years ago I was asked for an opinion by an attorney contemplating a lawsuit against an insurance company for inadequate replacement of a large diamond. His clients, a wealthy couple living in a fashionable condominium complex in Delray Beach, Florida, had been burglarized. The thieves stole a number of expensive items, including a three-and-a-half-carat round diamond in a platinum setting. The problem was that the only proof of the quality of the diamond the couple had was a photograph of the ring and a bill of sale from the jewelry store where they had purchased it. The stone was described as "a 3.50-carat round, brilliant-cut, white, clean diamond" on the original bill of sale. Using that description as a basis the insurance company replaced the stone with a 3.50-carat round, brilliant-cut, **poorly proportioned, yellowish (M color), heavily flawed (I2 clarity) diamond**. Needless to say, the couple was very upset with the insurance company's replacement and threatened legal action.

I asked a number of questions, including whether a professional appraiser had made a report on the quality of the diamond. I was given discouraging answers to each of my questions. Unfortunately the couple, although wealthy and sophisticated, did not have the evidentiary material to substantiate their claim as to the quality of the diamond. After examining all the relevant facts I concluded that if the attorney sued the insurance company, he would surely lose. The couple, because of a lack of proper documentation, unhappily had to accept the insurance company's replacement diamond.

Unfortunately, when it comes to insurance, it is easy to pay the premium for a policy but difficult to collect on a claim. This problem can be avoided with jewelry if the policy holder has credible documentation that proves the quality of the jewelry items that are insured. The key word here is "credible," because the jewelry report, called an appraisal, must come from a highly respectable source, not the corner retail jewelry store that may have sold you the merchandise originally. As I have previously mentioned, in my opinion the best documentary evidence you could have would be a Diamond Grading Report from the GIA. This report is the most respected description of the size, shape, and quality of your diamond available in North America. The report, properly used, is accepted by any insurance company, and, if need be, fully admissible in a court of law. In addition, if you have followed my advice and purchased a diamond that came with an authentic, corresponding GIA Diamond Grading Report, you can use this document for your insurance appraisal without incurring any additional costs.

The best way to register the quality of your diamond with your insurance company is to attach a photograph of the item, a copy of your bill of sale, which should included the number of the GIA Diamond Grading Report, and a photocopy of the actual GIA Diamond Grading Report to the insurance policy. Have your insurance agent sign off on the copies of these documents that you retain in your files. With these evidentiary materials attached to the policy there is little likelihood that there will be an argument at a time of loss.

If you have a diamond that does not have a corresponding GIA Diamond Grading Report, I strongly suggest that you send your unmounted diamond to one of the GIA laboratories for analysis. The time and cost involved to obtain a GIA Diamond Grading Report are more than worth it just for the protection it provides from your insurance carrier.

Here is a helpful tip that should save you lots of money over the next twenty-five years. Insurance companies want you to insure your jewelry at a monetary value. The higher the monetary value you put on a piece of jewelry the more premium you pay for that insurance. In the case of jewelry, the insurance company wants you to insure the goods at the *retail replacement cost*. This amount is equal to the price you would have to pay if you purchased the jewelry in a retail store. As you now know, retail prices are very high in comparison to wholesale prices. Therefore, the insurance company is trying to get you to insure your merchandise at the highest possible value to be able to charge you the highest possible premium. Interestingly, in most insurance policies, the company has the option of either giving you dollars or replacing the merchandise. Insurance companies know how to buy merchandise at the wholesale level. If you insure your jewelry at the retail price they will certainly opt to replace your merchandise because it is cheaper for them to do so. If you insure your merchandise at the wholesale level or below they will elect to give you dollars because it is cheaper for them to do so. Therefore, now that you know what the wholesale price is for your diamond, or have the knowledge to obtain that price, it is cheaper for you to insure your jewelry at the wholesale price and pay a cheaper premium every year that you renew your policy. The only thing you need to do is check the wholesale price of your stone every year or two to be sure that you're not underinsuring your jewelry.

CHAPTER 14

How to Sell a Diamond

Sometimes it is necessary or desirable to sell a diamond. An engagement might not work out, or an older couple might decide to sell a diamond because they need the money or want to avoid an inheritance dispute between their children. Most people sell their diamonds for a fraction of what they are really worth. After you read this chapter you will probably make a small profit or, at worst, get your money back, providing you bought the diamond correctly in the first place.

There are a number of commonsense rules you can follow to maximize the number of dollars you can obtain by selling your diamond. The most important rule is to know how much money your diamond is worth on the wholesale level. It is impossible to sell your diamond for top dollar unless you know what it is worth. It is like saying that you're going to become a physician without going to medical school. It just doesn't work that way.

If you own a diamond that has a corresponding GIA Diamond Grading Report, it is relatively easy to obtain the current wholesale price of the stone. All that is necessary is to look at the corresponding shape, size, and quality on a current Rapaport Diamond Report to determine the wholesale New York cash asking price. If you do not have a GIA Diamond Grading Report for your stone I strongly advise you to obtain one. Even though this report is going to cost you time and money, it is an extremely valuable document to have. The report will analyze the genuineness, size, and quality of the diamond you want to sell. In addition it will allow you to determine the wholesale price of the stone as well as demonstrate to any potential buyer that you know what you are doing and will not accept a ridiculously low price for your diamond.

Now that you know what your diamond is worth on the wholesale level, the all-important question is, where do you sell it? The traditional and easiest approach is to sell it to a diamond dealer, jewelry manufacturer, retail jeweler, or pawnbroker. If you are pressed for time or do not feel like expending much effort to sell your stone, this approach will work. Understand from the very beginning, however, that this easy avenue will not get you the maximum price for your diamond. The best way to sell your diamond to a jeweler or pawnbroker is to let him examine your stone and make you an offer first. Do not tell him you have a GIA Diamond Grading Report or know what the Rapaport diamond price is. Let him do all the talking. After he is finished making his offer, do not get offended. It is his job to try and buy the stone at the cheapest possible price. That's just business! It is your job to be informed. Next show him the GIA report and tell him the Rapaport price. Now the bargaining begins. Probably the best you can hope for is 50 percent of the Rapaport price for your diamond. These people are in business to make money. If they cannot buy significantly below the wholesale price, they will not spend their cold hard cash. That is their right and they will exercise it.

If I were not pressed for time, I would not sell the diamond to a jeweler or pawnshop. I would try to sell the stone privately. This is the best way to sell your diamond for the wholesale price plus the additional expenses you incurred, such as the cost of advertising and the GIA report. There are always private customers interested in purchasing diamonds for a reasonable price.

I would advertise the diamond in the classified advertisements of your local newspaper during the weekend. Normally there is a watch and jewelry section that interested buyers read. I would describe the size, shape, and quality of the stone without listing a price. Instead of giving the actual asking price I would use the word "Sacrifice" because it draws attention. My advertisement might look like the following example:

ESTATE SALE

A beautiful 1.10-carat round, brilliant-cut diamond, J color, SI2 clarity with GIA certificate.

Must sell. Sacrifice. (305) 555–0947

Another area that I would look at is the Internet. This electronic phenomenon is the most dynamic way to get your message to millions of people daily. Many of the providers, such as America Online, have electronic classified sections that are very effective. The advertisement is usually free if you are a subscriber.

I would use the same advertisement as in the previous example. If someone called from a distant location I would send them the diamond by registered insured mail after they sent money by wire transfer to your bank for the agreed upon price of the diamond. Do not accept checks of any kind! If the customer is not happy with the diamond once he has it evaluated he can have his money refunded per your agreement. If the diamond were returned it would be your responsibility to be certain that the stone had not been damaged or switched. This would require going to an expert gemologist-appraiser with the stone and the GIA diamond grading report and checking the stone before returning the money.

Lastly, if you sell the diamond in person be sure to accept payment in a safe place. It is all too easy for someone to agree to purchase your stone, pay you, and then have an accomplice rob you before you reach your home or bank. Therefore, the safest way to receive payment for your diamond is to have the purchaser meet you at your bank. Again, do not accept checks of any kind! To further ensure your safety, arrange to have the diamond stored in a safety deposit box inside the bank. That will prevent the possibility of being robbed of your diamond on your way to the bank for your appointment. You may think that I am being overly cautious or melodramatic, but when it comes to diamonds and precious metals you cannot be too vigilant. These commodities are just like money, and jewel thieves always know just where to go to turn stolen merchandise into cash. Furthermore, recovery is very unlikely because diamonds are easily shipped to another city, state, or country, and precious metals are almost always melted down and reused. To quote an old cliché, "A word to the wise should be sufficient!"

Another option is to sell the merchandise through an auction house. The first important consideration when thinking of working with an auction house is to know if they are honest and reliable. If we are discussing a world-renowned auction house such as Christie's or Sotheby's, there is no question about their integrity. However, a small local auction house that is relatively new in business should be eyed suspiciously before entrusting it with an expensive piece of jewelry. What happens if they close the door and disappear with your goods or refuse to pay you after they sell your piece? Your only legal recourse is to sue them, and that will take time, cost money, and may not lead to a successful outcome.

An additional problem associated with selling through an auction house is controlling the minimum price for which the item will be sold. This is called a "reserve price," and you must be sure that the auction house you are working with sells with reserve or minimum prices. If you do make an arrangement, be certain to get the terms in writing, with a valid signature of an officer of the company. Normally I do not recommend selling jewelry through an auction house because there are too many risks involved.

I do not like leaving merchandise with a jeweler on consignment. The primary reason is that the jeweler will not be anxious to sell consignment merchandise because he hasn't invested money in the piece. If the jeweler buys a diamond, he has a vested interest in selling that diamond not only to make a profit but also to get back his original investment. If he sells your diamond as opposed to his own, he will still be stuck with his inventory. I know this to be true because I used to give out consignment merchandise. For example, during the Christmas season I would sell a jeweler $20,000 worth of merchandise. Trying to push extra sales, I would then allow him to take $10,000 worth of goods on consignment. My thinking was that if I gave him extra merchandise, he would sell it and would not buy additional stock from my competitors. In reality what happened was the jeweler sold what he purchased and didn't push the consignment goods unless he had to. It was in his vested interest to sell what he bought, regardless of who the supplier was, and the rest was just used as window dressing. After a few years I stopped giving consignment pieces unless I was specifically asked to. It didn't pay.

Another problem with selling on consignment is that your merchandise may not be insured under the terms of the jeweler's insurance policy. What this means is that if he has a robbery or burglary, your merchandise may not be covered and you will have a difficult time getting paid by the jeweler. As a general rule, I do not think consigning diamonds or jewelry to a jeweler is a good idea and I would not use this approach.

CHAPTER 15

How Jewelry Is Manufactured

The purpose of this chapter is to give you an elementary understanding of the various processes employed in modern jewelry manufacturing. This will allow you to appreciate how the wholesale prices of fine jewelry are determined.

The ideal jewelry manufacturer has the complete staff required to produce, sell, distribute, and protect the fine jewelry produced in the factory. The model factory would be divided into four distinct branches: the production department, where the fine jewelry is fabricated; the marketing department, where the products are promoted and sold; the distribution department, where merchandise is shipped; and the security department, which protects the physical plant and merchandise against theft.

The production department is divided into a number of specialized sections that reflect the technologies used in manufacturing jewelry. In this example, the factory is going to make fine gold and silver rings, earrings, bracelets, charms, and pendants using the *lost-wax casting process*.

The first step in fabricating any new piece of jewelry is to design the new model. The *designer* sketches the new model in detailed drawings called *renderings* which depict the front, side, and top views of the model.

The *model maker*, following the renderings of the new model precisely, will hand make the design in a metal such as gold or silver or sculpt the new design using modeling wax. Regardless of the material initially used, the end result will be a finished *master* made in metal.

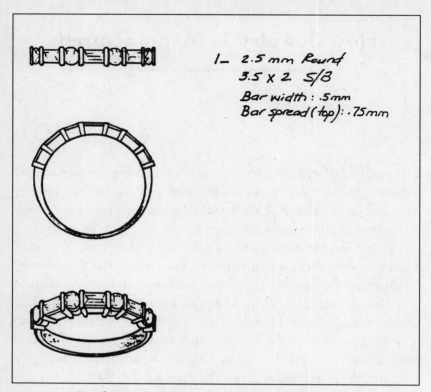

1— 2.5 mm Round
3.5 x 2 5/8
Bar width : .5mm
Bar spread (top): .75mm

Renderings. Models courtesy of Clara Weinerth

The master is given to the *mold maker*, who uses it to make a rubber mold. This mold is made by placing the master model between layers of vulcanized rubber and heating the material under pressure. The result is a block of bonded rubber which is then specially cut into two parts. The master model is removed. The mold consists of two solid pieces of rubber with an empty cavity. This cavity is an exact reproduction of the master model.

It is now possible to obtain many exact duplicate wax patterns of the original master from the rubber mold. This is accomplished in the *wax reproduction* section, where operators use pressurized wax injectors to shoot molten wax into the rubber

After the ring size has been selected, a Ring Gage (Fig. 1) is used for the initial "wax-up" of the custom ring.

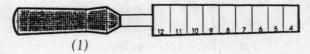

(1)

Pre-formed Wax Rods (Fig. 2) are placed in the area of the ring size. The wax rod is cut, and luted together with a hot wax spatula. (Fig. 3)

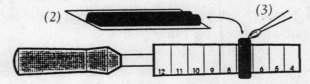

Custom designs are then formed by adding wax to the initial wax rod, using a wax spatula. (Fig. 4)

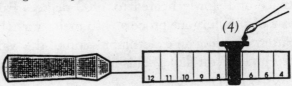

The wax pattern (Fig. 5) is removed from the Ring Gage and is now ready to be replaced by Gold, or any precious metal by the "lost-wax" casting procedure.

After the ring is cast and polished, the stone is set. (Fig. 6)

Simple Procedure for Custom-Designed Rings.
Courtesy of Dr. Melvin Poveromo

mold. When the wax cools, the rubber mold is opened and an exact wax reproduction of the original model is removed. It is important to understand that the same rubber mold may be used repeatedly to obtain as many patterns of the master design as desired. Inevitably the rubber mold will wear out, but another mold may be made as long as the original metal master is available. It is the process of mold making and the ability to make copies of the original design easily and inexpensively that are the keys to modern, mass-produced, lost-wax casted jewelry. This process revolutionized the jewelry industry because it allowed beautiful jewelry designs to be inexpensively reproduced and manufactured at affordable prices.

The next step in the process is the *burnout procedure*. The desired wax pattern is placed in a stainless-steel flask and wet plaster of Paris–type material called casting investment is poured on top of it. After the investment solidifies, the flask is placed into a furnace and slowly heated to 1400 degrees Fahrenheit. The purpose of the burnout process is to melt away (burn out) the wax pattern, leaving an exact impression of the wax pattern in the cured investment flasks. This is why this process is called the lost-wax casting process.

We are now ready to *cast*. Casting is the process where molten metal is injected into the burned-out flasks. The metal will fill the empty cavity in the flask and when the flask is cooled and opened there will be an exact metallic reproduction of the burned-out wax pattern. Modern-day jewelry manufacturers use centrifugal and vacuum casting machines to force the molten metal into the empty cavities of the burned-out flask. The hot flask is then placed into water until the investment (plaster) breaks apart and the rough metallic forms are removed.

The lost-wax casting method described in the factory above is very popular today because of its versatility, economy, and mass production capability. This technique is normally used to manufacture solid jewelry such as rings, which require structural strength to retain their shape and wear well.

When a metallic casting is removed from the burned-out flask it is in an unfinished condition. The piece of jewelry called a casting may require sawing, filing, shaping, repairing, assembling, and soldering. These functions are performed in the *jeweler's department*, where skilled craftsmen will work on the casting until it approaches a nearly finished condition.

If the design of the jewelry requires diamonds or colored stones to be added, the next step in the manufacturing process is the *stone setting department*. This is where expert artisans known as setters place the stones securely in the jewelry.

After the stones have been set it is time to finish the piece by polishing the metal. This is accomplished in the *polishing department*. Here craftsmen carefully polish the metal to bring out its deep and lustrous shine, eliminating any surface flaws or blemishes. In some instances, the jewelry is gold or rhodium plated to further enhance its appearance.

Normally the jewelry is then sent to the *quality control section*, where inspectors carefully examine it for defects. Once the piece has passed inspection it is sent to the *distribution department* for shipment to the customer.

Depending on the characteristics of the jewelry being produced there are other technologies that modern manufacturers use. For example, in the production of hollow, lightweight earrings the manufacturer normally employs the *metal stamping process*. Specific metal forms called dies are made to reproduce certain shapes such as two opposite halves of an earring. When the die is finished, it is used in conjunction with a machine called a stamping press. This press has the ability to exert tremendous pressure on the steel die. As gold, silver, or platinum passes through the steel die the pressure exerted by the press forms the needed shape. In the case of hollow earrings two oppo-

Two basic items that are used in the laboratory for casting by way of the "lost-wax" technique are:

(7) Casting Ring (Stainless Steel Cylinder) ⟶

(8) Rubber Sprue Former ⟶

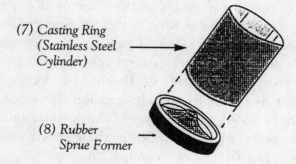

The wax pattern of the ring (Fig. 9) is placed into the Sprue Former and attached by means of a Wax Sprue. (Fig. 10)

The Casting Ring is placed over the Sprue Former. (Fig. 11)

(9) ⟶

(10) ⟶

(11) ⟶

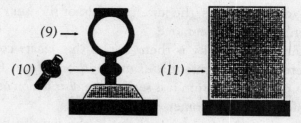

The Casting Ring is then filled with a soft mixture of Casting Investment.

Once hardened, it is similar in texture to Plaster of Paris.

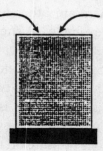

Casting Procedure—Lost-Wax Technique.
Courtesy of Dr. Melvin Poveromo

After the investment has hardened, the Sprue Former is removed.

The Sprue Channel which will receive the Molten Metal (after the wax has evaporated) is shown. (Fig. 12)

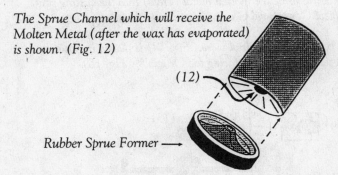

(12)

Rubber Sprue Former ⟶

The Casting Ring is then placed in a Heated Oven at approximately 1400 degrees F for a prescribed amount of time.

During this time, the wax pattern will melt and evaporate until the chamber is void of all the wax.

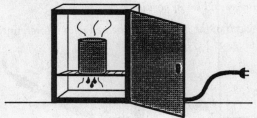

A cross section of the Casting Ring demonstrates the recess or chamber that is left after the wax has evaporated.

During casting procedures, the molten metal will enter the opening at the end (Fig. 13) and continue through the sprue channel to the end of the mold.

(13)

In order to force the molten metal (Gold) into the casting ring, a typical Centrifugal Casting Machine is shown.

The casting ring (sagittal view - Fig. 14) is placed in position with the sprue opening facing the Crucible. (Fig. 15)

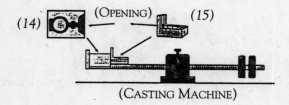

(14)   (OPENING)   (15)

(CASTING MACHINE)

Sequence:

(A) The arm of the casting machine (which is spring wound) is rotated several times, and set in position.

(B) Gold is placed in the crucible and heated with a torch until it is molten. (Fig. 16)

(16)

(C) When the arm of the Casting Machine is released, the entire unit spins in a counter-clockwise direction, forcing the molten Gold to enter the opening of the casting ring into the mold, thereby "casting" the ring.

The Casting Ring is removed from the Casting Machine and allowed to cool until the Gold solidifies.

The casting investment (containing the ring mold) is separated from the casting ring. The investment is removed from the Gold Ring by various methods, including "sand blasting."

The Sprue is cut off (Fig. 17), and the ring is polished (Fig. 18).

(17)   (18)

After the ring is polished, "finger-like" prongs are soldered in the appropriate areas to receive the emerald cut stone.

A final polish is applied to the ring, and the stone is set.

site forms are manufactured. These opposite forms are then permanently joined by soldering (fusing) them together into one earring. The jewelry and polishing work is then performed to finish the stamped hollow earrings.

Automatic weaving equipment has been developed by the jewelry industry to manufacture machine-made, mass-produced chains. These machines use wire and plates of different sizes and thicknesses that automatically turn and twist the soft metal until the desired shape is created. After a spool of chain has been fabricated, which may be 50 to 100 feet in length, it is cut by machine to the desired length. The clasp system, which holds both ends of the chain together around the neck, wrist, or ankle, is then soldered to the two ends of the chain. The soldered chain may be sent to the jeweler's department for additional work, or it may be sent to the polishing department for polishing and/or plating.

In many instances more than one manufacturing process is used to complete a piece of jewelry. In our previous example of the fabrication of a chain we employ two separate processes. To make the length of the chain the weaving machinery is used, but the lock, called a clasp, that holds the two ends of the chain together may be either cast by the lost-wax process or stamped using metal dies and a stamping press.

In making many different styles of earrings the main body may be stamped, cast, or woven, but the mechanism that attaches the earring to the ear, called a post, normally is stamped.

In diamond engagement rings the main part of the ring, called the shank, is normally cast, but the parts that hold the diamond(s), called heads or prongs, are usually stamped.

At this point you should have a basic understanding of the various processes involved in manufacturing fine jewelry. Equally important from the educated consumer's point of view is a rudimentary understanding of the different types of crafts and mer-

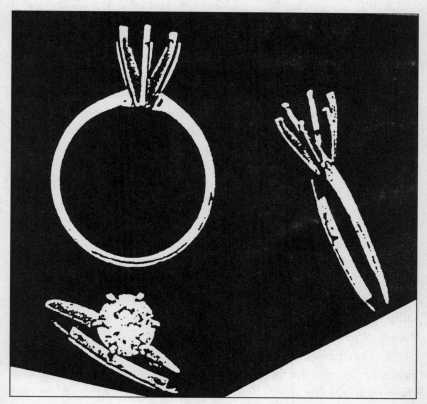

Engagement Ring

chants that comprise the jewelry industry. The following list, although not complete, represents those members of the jewelry trade with whom you may come in contact if you wish to purchase on the wholesale level.

1. Designer—A jewelry designer is an artist who develops a preliminary plan or sketch for a new model. This sketch of the new pattern is called a rendering.

2. Model Maker—A jewelry model maker is an artisan who fabricates by hand the new model from the designer's rendering.

This model may be made in a metal such as silver or gold or carved from modeling wax.

3. Mold Maker—A mold maker is a craftsperson who uses the casted, metallic master to manufacture one or more rubber molds that are used in the lost-wax casting process.

4. Caster—A caster reproduces a metal form from a wax pattern by using the lost-wax process. A caster normally cuts rubber molds, makes wax patterns, and produces metallic replicas of the wax patterns.

5. Jeweler—A jeweler is a craftsperson who knows how to work with precious metal. Typically, a jeweler will file, saw, grind, solder, and assemble a rough casting and make it into a semi-finished model ready for additional finishing work. In addition, jewelers perform sizings, various repairs, and remodeling to metallic jewelry pieces.

6. Setter—A setter is a artisan who safely, securely, aesthetically, and permanently attaches gemstones such as diamonds to pieces of jewelry.

7. Polisher—A polisher is a tradesperson who finishes the piece of jewelry by brightening the metal to a radiant shine, thereby removing minor faults and blemishes. The polisher may also plate the piece of jewelry to enhance its appearance.

8. Diamond Dealer—On the wholesale level, a diamond dealer is a merchant who sells diamonds to manufacturers, retailers, or other diamond dealers. Most large diamond dealers, in order to be competitively priced, import large quantities of diamonds from overseas cutting centers such as Israel, Belgium, and India or cut and polish the diamonds themselves domestically.

9. Fine Jewelry Dealer—On the wholesale level, the fine jewelry dealer is a merchant who sells fine jewelry, usually by weight, to retailers or to other dealers. Normally a gold or silver jewelry dealer imports merchandise from another country but

may also buy large quantities of merchandise from domestic manufacturers at discounted prices.

10. Findings Dealer—Jewelry findings are standard parts used in the assembly or manufacture of jewelry such as manufactured locks, clasps, earring backs, and certain forms of pre-shaped heads used for setting diamonds. On the wholesale level, a findings dealer is a merchant who sells findings to manufacturers, repair jewelers, and other findings dealers.

11. Jewelry Manufacturer—A jewelry manufacturer is a person or company that fabricates jewelry or produces some parts for jewelry (e.g. findings). Due to the ability to contract out various stages of the manufacturing process, such as casting or setting, the size and structure of jewelry manufacturing companies vary. Manufacturers normally sell their products to retailers or wholesale merchants.

There is a bottom-line lesson to this chapter that is very important for you to remember because it has a very direct effect on present-day jewelry pricing. Historically, jewelry was laboriously made, one piece at a time, by hand. No automation of any type existed and therefore fine jewelry was reserved for only the wealthy. With the arrival of the twentieth-century's technological innovations jewelry manufacturing was converted from an expensive, low volume, labor intensive trade to a highly mechanized, large volume, popularly priced industry. Today mass-produced jewelry using such technologies as the lost-wax casting process, stamping, and automated chain making machines account for nearly 100 percent of the fine jewelry manufactured in the United States and Canada. Consequently, uniquely designed, totally handmade pieces of jewelry are almost unknown and labor costs are not as significant a factor when calculating the wholesale price of fine jewelry.

CHAPTER 16

How Wholesale Prices of Gold Chains Are Determined

There are three primary elements that determine the wholesale prices of precious metal jewelry. Once you understand these underlying economic realities you will be able to calculate the approximate wholesale price of any piece of fine jewelry made only from precious metal and devoid of stones. It will not matter if you are purchasing a gold, platinum, or silver piece because the fundamental considerations are always the same.

The wholesale price of fine jewelry is determined by:

1. The precious metal content of the piece;
2. The various costs incurred in manufacturing the piece;
3. The costs involved in distributing the jewelry until it becomes available to you for sale.

I am going to use the purchase of a gold chain to demonstrate how to purchase fine jewelry. Remember, however, that these principles will hold true for the purchase of rings, earrings, pendants, charms, brooches, or any other type of mass-produced commercial jewelry that is available for sale in any of the other precious metals (platinum or silver).

It has been estimated that most North Americans own at least one gold chain that is worn around the neck. Because of their popularity and price, chains are the most frequently purchased type of karat gold jewelry. Today, most chains are manufactured by automated chain-making (weaving) machines in foreign countries. Italy manufactures and exports more chains than any other nation due to their superior styling and expert finishing techniques.

The most important factor in determining the wholesale price of a gold chain is the weight of the fine gold content. It is similar to buying bananas at a produce market in that the more they weigh the more they cost. To understand how to properly purchase a gold chain, or any other gold item for that matter, it is necessary to understand a few basic facts about gold and how it is measured.

Gold in its purest form is devoid of all other metals. In this state pure gold is also called fine gold, or 24-karat gold. When gold is this pure it is very soft and easily bends out of shape. Normally 24-karat gold is too soft to be used in jewelry.

In the manufacture of jewelry, pure gold is melted together with other metals to give it additional strength. The more metal that is added to the pure gold, the harder the gold becomes. Jewelers do not want gold to become as hard as steel, so there are accepted limits to the amount of metals that are added. When other metals are melted together with pure gold the method is called alloying the gold. The metals that are added to the gold are called *alloy*. Gold that includes alloy is called *karat gold*.

In North America there are three classifications of alloyed gold that are widely accepted in jewelry. They are 18-karat gold, 14-karat gold, and 10-karat gold. To understand what these designations mean, it is important to remember that pure gold is 24-karat gold or 24 parts gold with no other metal present.

Eighteen-karat gold is composed of 18 parts pure gold and 6 parts alloy metal. That means that 75 percent of the metal is pure gold and 25 percent of the metal is alloy. If you divide 18 by 24 you will get .750 or 75 percent.

Fourteen-karat gold is composed of 14 parts pure gold and 10 parts alloy. That means that 58.34 percent of the metal is pure gold and 41.66 percent of the metal is alloy. If you divide 14 by 24 you will get .5834 or 58.34 percent.

Ten-karat gold is composed of 10 parts pure gold and 14 parts alloy. That means that 41.66 percent of the metal is pure gold and 58.34 percent of the metal is alloy. If you divide 10 by 24 you will get .4166 or 41.66 percent.

GOLD CONTENT AND HALLMARKS

HALLMARK (USA)	PARTS	GOLD PERCENTAGE	HALLMARK (EUROPEAN)
24K	24/24	99.9 percent	999
18K	18/24	75.0 percent	750
14K	14/24	58.3 percent	585
10K	10/24	41.6 percent	417

A 14-karat gold neck chain is composed of 14 parts pure gold and 10 parts alloy. The total amount of pure gold in the chain should be 58.34 percent of the weight of the chain.

In order to determine the value of a chain we need to be able to weigh it. The most precise system for weighing gold is the metric system. The unit of measurement that is used in the metric system for weighing gold is a gram. There are 31.1035 grams to a metric ounce. The other system that is used for weighing gold is *troy weight*. Here the unit of measurement is a *pennyweight*. There are 20 pennyweights in a troy ounce. The problem with the troy weight is that it is less precise than the metric system because there are fewer units of measure to the ounce. Consequently, if you are weighing gold, you want to insist on weighing it in grams and not pennyweights.

At this point you are ready to calculate the gold value of a chain you are thinking of purchasing. The chain is 14-karat gold and weighs 20 grams. A current price of pure gold is $400 per ounce. In the metric system there are 31.1035 grams in an ounce. Therefore if you divide $400 by 31.1035 grams you will obtain the price of 1 gram of *pure or 24-karat gold*. After doing the mathematics you know that a gram of pure gold is worth

$12.86. You also know that 14-karat gold is comprised of 58.34 percent pure gold. If you multiply the price of pure gold per gram by the 14-karat percentage (58.34 percent) you will obtain the price of a gram of 14-karat gold, which is $7.50. In order to determine the value of the gold content of the chain you are considering purchasing, you multiply the price per gram of 14-karat gold by the total weight of the chain. The gold value of a 14-karat gold chain weighing 20 grams when the price of pure gold is $400 would be $150.

The mathematics for this example would be:

1. $400 (the current price of pure gold per ounce) divided by 31.1035 (the number of grams to a metric ounce) equals $12.86 (the price of one gram of pure gold);

2. $12.86 multiplied by .5834 (14-karat gold percentage) equals $7.50 (the price of 14-karat gold);

3. $7.50 multiplied by 20 grams (the weight of the chain) equals $150 (the gold value or intrinsic value of the chain).

At this point we have the gold or intrinsic value of this chain if the price of gold is $400 per ounce. If the price of gold goes up or down the intrinsic value of the chain will go up or down accordingly.

There are additional factors that come into play when determining the wholesale price of this chain. The first consideration is how much the chain cost to manufacture. Here we have to consider factors such as the operating overhead of the factory, the cost of alloy metals, the machine time required to manufacture the chain, and profit for the manufacturer. As a rule of thumb you should add an additional 25 to 30 percent to the price of the chain for the manufacturing cost and profit.

Next, the company that imports and/or distributes the chain on the wholesale level must be considered. They also have overhead expenses like rent, salaries, taxes, travel, customs duties, etc., and they are entitled to make a profit for their efforts. Once again the rule of thumb is a 25 to 30 percent markup from the price at which they purchased the chain from the manufacturer.

Therefore, if the gold value of the chain is $7.50 per gram and the manufacturer adds 30 percent for his services, the chain will be sold to the importer/wholesaler for $9.75 per gram. In addition, if the wholesaler adds another 30 percent, the price per gram of this 14-karat gold chain will be $14.63 per gram. This chain, weighing 20 grams, will have a wholesale price of approximately $292.60. That is $142.60 above the gold or intrinsic value of the chain.

The retailer then normally marks the chain up at least 200 percent. This will make the retail price of the chain approximately $875. Depending on the retailer's pricing policies, the chain can be left at full retail, marked down, put on sale, etc. The important point to remember is that the intrinsic or gold value is what the chain is actually worth and everything else represents costs which under normal circumstances you can never recover.

As a general rule, if you are considering purchasing a gold chain it is reasonable to spend between 50 to 60 percent above the intrinsic gold value of that chain. In my opinion, anything above that price is excessive.

You can avoid having to go through these lengthy mathematical procedures by using Appendix A, which consists of charts of the per gram price of 10-, 14-, and 18-karat gold. These charts are based on the price of pure or 24-karat gold starting at $150 per ounce and moving in $10 increments up to $800 per ounce. Simply multiply the correct per gram value by the total gram weight to calculate the total gold value of the chain.

I have previously mentioned that the troy weight system is not as accurate as the metric system and should be avoided whenever possible. The troy weight system uses pennyweight as its standard. There are 20 pennyweights to a troy ounce. Therefore if the current price of pure gold is $400 per ounce then the per pennyweight price of pure gold is $20. The 14-karat gold price per pennyweight would be $11.67. The same 20-gram, 14-karat gold chain used in the previous example would weigh 13 pennyweights. The gold value of the same chain using the troy weight system is $151.71, a difference of $1.71 against you.

The mathematics for the previous example would be:

1. $400 (current price of pure gold) divided by 20 pennyweights equals $20 (the price of a pennyweight of pure gold);

2. $20 multiplied by .5834 (the percentage of 14-karat gold) equals $11.67 (the price of a pennyweight of 14-karat gold);

3. $11.67 multiplied by 13 pennyweights (the weight of the chain) equals $151.71 (the gold or intrinsic value of the chain).

You may run into a situation where you need to convert from metric to troy or vice versa. The following formulae are used to convert a weight from pennyweight to grams or from grams to pennyweights.

1. To convert from metric (grams) to troy (pennyweights) divide the gram amount by the constant 1.555. Example: Convert 20 grams to the equivalent weight in pennyweights. *20 grams divided by 1.555 equals 12.861 pennyweights.*

2. To convert from troy (pennyweights) to metric (grams) multiply the pennyweight amount by the constant 1.555 to convert to grams. Example: Convert 12.861 pennyweights to grams. *12.861 multiplied by 1.555 equals 20 grams.*

Appendix B has a number of other examples of how to determine the gold value of jewelry for those readers who either enjoy mathematical problems or want additional practice figuring out the gold value of chains.

CHAPTER 17

Calculating the Wholesale Prices of Gold Jewelry

All modern, mass-produced, commercial gold jewelry is formed by machines. Rings, charms, earrings, bracelets, and brooches may be cast, stamped, or woven by machines. Due to this manner of manufacture it is possible to determine wholesale prices quite easily.

RINGS

The most frequently used method of manufacturing rings is the lost-wax casting method. Some standard rings that are manufactured in large quantities, such as four-prong engagement rings, may be stamped. Regardless of the method used, the rings will require some jewelry work in order to finish them. In the case of a cast ring a jeweler will clean the rough casting and possibly assemble and repair it. The proper sizing of the ring could have been performed in the wax prior to casting, but the size may be altered by a jeweler. The ring is then polished and possibly plated by a polisher. Thus a finished casted ring without any gemstones is processed by a caster, a jeweler, and a polisher.

A fair wholesale price for a ring weighing between one and five grams is the intrinsic gold value plus 150-percent processing charges. The charge for any ring over five grams is the intrinsic gold value plus a 125-percent processing charge. The reason there is a difference in processing charges is because the labor to manufacture each ring is exactly the same but the lighter rings have less weight to charge for. To make up for this discrepancy there is an additional premium for lighter goods. This principle holds true for most types of commercial, mass-produced jewelry.

Therefore if pure gold is presently priced at $500 per ounce, a 14-karat gold ring weighing six grams should cost approximately $126.66. I calculated this price as follows:

1. The fine gold price ($500) is divided by 31.1035 (grams in a metric ounce) equaling $16.08 per gram;

2. $16.08 is multiplied by .5834 (14-karat gold percentage) equalling $9.38 per gram for 14-karat gold (at $500 per ounce fine gold);

3. $9.38 per gram multiplied by 125 percent (processing charge) equals $11.73 per gram;

4. Add $9.38 (14-karat per gram price) plus $11.73 (processing charge) equals $21.11 total per gram charge;

5. $21.11 per gram multiplied by 6 grams equals $126.66 (total wholesale price of the ring).

CHARMS

There are thousands of different styles of trinkets that can be worn on a chain or bracelet. Most charms, including religious medallions, are either cast or stamped. They are generally uncomplicated, one-piece designs that do not require a great deal of skilled jewelry processing to complete. Gold charms are mass-market items that normally weigh between one and six grams. As a general rule you should not pay more than 125 percent above the intrinsic value of the gold content in a charm. For example, what would a charm cost if the current price of gold is $440 and the charm is made of 18-karat gold and weighs 4.50 grams? The way to determine the price is to first calculate the intrinsic value of the gold in the charm. This is done by determining the value of a gram of 18-karat gold and multiplying that value by 4.50 grams.

1. $440 per ounce divided by 31.1035 grams (number of grams in a metric ounce) equals $14.15 per gram of 24-karat (pure) gold;

2. 18-karat gold is 75 percent pure gold and 25 percent alloy (18 divided by 24 equals 75 percent or .75);

3. $14.15 multiplied by .75 (the percentage of fine gold in 18-karat gold) equals $10.61 per gram (the value of one gram of 18-karat gold);

4. $10.61 multiplied by 4.50 grams (the weight of the charm) equals $47.74 (intrinsic gold value of the charm).

At this point we know that the intrinsic gold value of the charm is $47.74. Now we have to include the 125 percent charge for manufacturing, overhead, and profit costs to the charm. Therefore the wholesale price of this charm would be $107.42. This is calculated by multiplying the intrinsic value of $47.74 by 2.25, equalling $107.42.

EARRINGS

Earrings are very popular, lightweight, mass-market items that are manufactured by stamping or by the casting process. Since earrings are always purchased in pairs, their cumulative weight generally ranges between two and ten grams. They can either be attached through a hole in the ear lobe (pierced ear system) or by a clip that holds them firmly to the ear lobe (clip-on system). The most widely used system in North America is the pierced ear system which employs either a post and butterfly or the more expensive screw back. Better quality diamond stud earrings employ the screw-back system because it offers greater protection against accidental loss.

For lighter weight earrings between one and five grams you should not pay more than 125 percent above the fine gold intrinsic value of the earrings. For earrings six grams and up you should not pay more than 100 percent above the fine gold intrinsic value. For stamped diamond stud earrings with a screw-back system you can pay 150 percent above the gold intrinsic value. For diamond stud earrings that use a post and butterfly system you should pay 125 percent above the gold intrinsic value. If I were buying a pair of diamond stud earrings I would only purchase the earrings that came with the screw-back system because the price differential is small but the earrings are almost impossible to lose.

As an example, say you are interested in purchasing a pair of 14-karat yellow gold hoop earrings that weigh a total of 6 grams and gold is presently priced at $385 per ounce. The wholesale price would be calculated as follows:

1. $385 divided by 31.1035 equals $12.38 per gram (the price of 24-karat gold);

2. $12.38 multiplied by .5833 equals $7.22 per gram (the price of 14-karat gold);

3. $7.22 multiplied by 2 equals $14.44 per gram (the price of 14-karat gold earrings 6 grams and over);

4. $14.44 multiplied by 6 grams equals $86.64 (the wholesale price of the 14-karat gold hoop earrings).

What would be the wholesale price of a pair of 18-karat white gold diamond stud earrings weighing 5 grams when the price of 24-karat gold is $410 per ounce?

1. $410 divided by 31.1035 equals $13.18 per gram (the price of 24-karat gold);

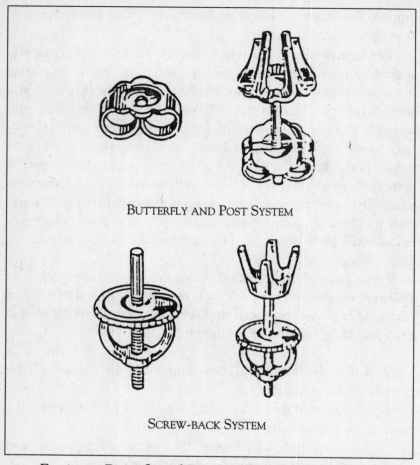

BUTTERFLY AND POST SYSTEM

SCREW-BACK SYSTEM

Earrings—Butterfly and Post System/Screw-Back System

2. $13.18 multiplied by .750 equals $9.89 per gram (the price of 18-karat gold);

3. $9.89 multiplied by 2.25 equals $22.25 per gram (the price of 18-karat gold earrings 5 grams and less);

4. $22.25 multiplied by 5 grams equals $111.25 (the wholesale price of 18-karat gold diamond stud earrings).

BRACELETS

There are many different varieties of fine gold bracelets that are manufactured by stamping, casting, or from automatic chain-making machines. They range in weight from very light to very heavy, depending upon the style, thickness, and length of the bracelet. As a general rule the wholesale price of a bracelet that weighs more than six grams is 100 percent above the gold intrinsic value. A bracelet that is less than six grams will wholesale for 125 percent above the gold intrinsic value. The wholesale price of a man's 10-karat nugget bracelet that weighs one ounce (31.1035 grams) when an ounce of pure gold costs $395 would be $329.07. This is calculated as follows:

1. $395 divided by 31.1035 equals $12.70 per gram (the price of 24-karat gold);
2. $12.70 multiplied by .4166 (the percentage of fine gold in 10-karat gold) equals $5.29 per gram (the price of 10-karat gold);
3. $5.29 multiplied by 2.00 equals $10.58 per gram (the price of 10-karat gold bracelet over 5 grams);
4. $10.58 multiplied by 31.1035 grams equals $329.07 (the wholesale price of a man's 10-karat gold nugget bracelet).

BROOCHES

A brooch is an ornament that is attached by a pin. They are normally manufactured by the lost-wax casting method even though large quantities of the same design may be fabricated by the stamping process. The unique aspect in the construction of a brooch is that it requires a pin and catch system. The more sophisticated systems are normally purchased from a findings house and soldered to the back of the brooch during the assembly process.

The pricing of a brooch is again dependent upon its weight. If it is lightweight, between one and six grams, using a stamped pin and catch system, its wholesale price will be its gold intrinsic value plus 125 percent. If it is a heavier piece, the price will be its gold intrinsic value plus 100 percent.

What would be the wholesale price of an 18-karat gold brooch that weighs 10 grams with the present price of pure gold at $445 per ounce? The price would be determined as follows:

1. $445 (price of one ounce) divided by 31.1035 grams (number of grams in an ounce) equals $14.30 per gram (the price of one gram of fine gold at $445 per ounce);

2. $14.30 divided by .750 (the percentage of fine gold in 18-karat gold) equals $10.73 (the price of one gram of 18-karat gold;

3. $10.73 multiplied by 10 grams (the weight of the brooch) equals $107.30 (the value of the fine gold in the brooch);

4. $107.30 multiplied by 2.00 (the additional 100 percent charge for manufacturing, labor, and profit) equals $214.60 (the total price of the brooch).

This brief summary of how various types of gold jewelry are priced on the wholesale level is meant as an overview. Other sundry items such as cuff links, belt buckles, tie tacks, etc., employ the same basic logic and calculations. What I have not taken into account are the various local, state, and federal taxes that may apply. These methods of determining wholesale prices work and you should be able to purchase your gold jewelry using this system. If you have problems matching these prices please contact me and I will try to help you.

CHAPTER 18

Calculating the Wholesale Prices of Platinum Jewelry

Platinum is a white metal that possesses a number of superb characteristics that make it very suitable for use in the manufacture of fine jewelry. It is a very hard metal that does not corrode, resists tarnishing, does not scratch easily, and is hypoallergenic. Due to its great strength and hardness it is an excellent metal for securing diamonds and other precious gemstones.

Unfortunately, along with its many positive qualities platinum has a number of serious disadvantages. Platinum has a very high melt temperature, which makes it far more difficult to cast and work on than gold jewelry. It is a very dense metal, making pieces of jewelry weigh far more than their gold counterparts. If a 14-karat white gold engagement set weighs 7 grams, the exact same set would weigh 11.55 grams in platinum (assuming a 90 percent platinum content). If an 18-karat white gold bracelet weighs 15 grams the same bracelet would weigh 21 grams in platinum (assuming a 90 percent platinum content).

Jewelry made from platinum is far more expensive than its gold counterparts for five basic reasons:

1. Platinum is normally more expensive than gold. As of the writing of this chapter gold was priced at $342.80 per ounce while platinum cost $388.40 per ounce;

2. Platinum jewelry contains a higher degree of purity than its gold counterparts. Platinum jewelry normally contains 90 percent platinum as compared to 75 percent gold in 18-karat or

58.35 percent gold in 14-karat jewelry. This higher degree of purity at a higher per ounce price makes platinum jewelry more expensive than gold;

3. The metal used to alloy platinum is far more expensive than the metals used to alloy gold. Iridium, ruthenium, palladium, and cobalt are all more expensive metals than silver, copper, zinc, and nickel, which are normally used to alloy gold;

4. Platinum jewelry is much heavier than its gold counterpart. Platinum is approximately 65 percent heavier than 14-karat gold and 40 percent heavier than 18-karat gold. Since the price is calculated by weight this factor alone would make platinum much costlier;

5. Because of its density, high melt temperature, and hardness platinum is a more difficult metal to cast and work on than its gold counterpart.

In order to calculate the wholesale price of a piece of platinum jewelry it is necessary to know the overall weight of the piece and how much platinum it contains. This is accomplished by understanding how to read the *hallmark* stamped inside the piece of jewelry. The following hallmarks are used for platinum jewelry and they specify the degree of purity that each piece of jewelry contains:

1. PLATINUM can be used on a piece of jewelry containing at least 95 percent platinum;

2. PLAT can be used on a piece of jewelry containing at least 95 percent platinum;

3. IRIDPLAT designates that at least 75 percent of the metal used is platinum and the balance is a platinum group alloy. For example, the hallmark 90%PLAT10%IRID means that 90 percent of the piece is made from platinum and it is alloyed with 10 percent iridium;

4. PLATINE designates that at least 95 percent of the metal used is platinum;

5. PT 1000 signifies that 100 percent of the metal used is platinum;

6. PT 950 means that 95 percent of the metal employed is platinum;

7. PT 900 denotes that 90 percent of the metal contained is platinum;

8. PT 850 specifies that 85 percent of the metal used is platinum.

RINGS

Let's assume that an engagement ring weighs 9 grams of PT 900 and the current price of platinum is $388.40. The wholesale price of this ring would be calculated as follows:

1. $388.40 (price per ounce of platinum) divided by 31.1035 grams (number of grams in a metric ounce) equals $12.49 (price per gram of platinum);

2. $12.49 multiplied by 9 grams (total weight of the ring) equals $112.38 (total intrinsic value of platinum contained in this ring). Actually .9 grams or 10 percent of the total weight of the ring is alloy which costs less than the platinum. For ease of calculation I have priced the entire ring at the platinum price, which will be a modest overstatement but for our present purposes this method is accurate enough.

3. Due to the inherent difficulties of casting and working in platinum the premium charge for casting, finishing, overhead, distribution, and profit is calculated at 150 percent. Therefore this ring could sell on the wholesale level for $281.96 plus tax. This is calculated by multiplying 2.50 (100 percent + 150 percent) by $112.38 (the intrinsic platinum value of the ring).

BRACELETS

A platinum diamond bracelet weighs 25 grams and contains 75 percent platinum and 25 percent palladium. The current cost of platinum is $410 per ounce and the cost of palladium is $140 per ounce. How much will this bracelet cost? The cost of this bracelet is calculated using the following steps:

1. $410 divided by 31.1035 equals $13.18 per gram of platinum;

2. $140 (price of an ounce of palladium) divided by 31.1035 equals $4.50 (price of a gram of palladium);

3. 25 grams (total weight of the bracelet) multiplied by .75 (percentage of platinum contained in bracelet) equals 18.75 grams (amount of platinum in grams);

4. 25 grams multiplied by .25 (percentage of palladium contained in bracelet) equals 6.25 grams (amount of palladium in grams);

5. 18.75 grams of platinum multiplied by $13.18 equals $247.13 worth of platinum;

6. 6.25 grams of palladium multiplied by $140 equals $28.13 worth of palladium;

7. $247.13 + $28. 13 = $275.26 (total intrinsic value of platinum and palladium of the bracelet);

8. $275.26 multiplied by 2.50 (100 percent + 150 percent) equals $688.15, the total wholesale cost of the bracelet plus tax. This price includes a 150 percent premium charge for casting, finishing, overhead, distribution, and profit. What is not included is the price for setting any diamonds or gemstones. This charge can vary between $5 per stone to hundreds of dollars, depending on the method of setting and the size of the stone.

In conclusion, it is basically easy to calculate the wholesale price for a piece of platinum jewelry if you know the per-ounce price for the platinum and its alloys, the weight of the piece of jewelry, and use 150 percent as a premium charge. If the piece is very lightweight, less than 5 grams, a premium charge of 200 percent is used.

CHAPTER 19

Calculating the Wholesale Prices
of Silver Jewelry

Pure silver is an almost white metal that is too soft to be used in jewelry. To increase the strength of silver so it will not distort or wear out quickly it is normally alloyed with copper. Sterling silver is the most common combination of alloyed silver where $7^{1}/_{2}$ percent of copper is added to $92^{1}/_{2}$ percent pure silver. Therefore, if a piece of sterling silver jewelry weighed 10 grams then 9.25 grams would be fine silver and .75 gram would be copper. The hallmark for sterling silver is .925.

Mexican silver is another less frequently used alloyed combination in which the pure silver content is normally 90 percent. Many of the pieces that are imported from Mexico and other Third World countries are stamped .900, which is the hallmark for Mexican silver.

According to Silver Trust International, a trade group located in New York that promotes the use and sale of silver for jewelry, flatware, and the gift industries, the retail sales of sterling silver jewelry in 1995 were estimated at 1.85 billion dollars. The United States consumes nearly 15 million troy ounces of silver in the form of jewelry each year and almost 85 percent of that amount is imported from other countries, notably from Thailand, Italy, and Mexico.

Sixty percent of the sterling silver jewelry buyers in 1995 were women purchasing for themselves. The most popular items were earrings, which accounted for one-third of all purchases; neckwear, which accounted for 25 percent of the entire sales; and rings and bracelets, which represented approximately 20 percent each of the remaining sales. The average retail price paid per sterling silver jewelry item in 1995 was $38.

At the time of the writing of this chapter the price of pure silver is $4.83 per ounce. To determine the wholesale price of a commercial, mass-produced piece of sterling silver jewelry it is necessary to know the actual or intrinsic value of the fine silver contained in the piece. For example, what would be the intrinsic value of the fine silver contained in an imported, machine-made, sterling silver necklace that weighs 25 grams when the price of pure silver is $4.83 per ounce? To determine the answer it is necessary to perform the following calculations:

1. $4.83 (price per ounce of fine silver) divided by 31.1035 grams (number of grams in an ounce) equals $.155 (price per gram of fine silver);
2. 25 grams (the weight of the chain) multiplied by .925 (the percentage of fine silver in sterling silver) equals 23.125 grams of fine silver;
3. 23.125 grams (amount of fine silver in the necklace) multiplied by $.155 (the per gram price of fine silver) equals $3.84.

The 25-gram imported necklace contains a total of $3.84 worth of fine silver. However the wholesale price for this necklace might be as high as $28.34. The reason is that the cost of manufacturing, distributing, shipping charges, import duties, overhead, and profit is significantly higher than the cost of the sterling silver used to make the jewelry. The other interesting factor is that the manufacturing process for making a necklace or ring is almost identical regardless of whether the manufacturer is using $400 an ounce gold or $4 per ounce silver.

In some cases a piece of silver jewelry that has relatively little intrinsic value can cost $100 or more. The reason is that it is manufactured by a well-known designer or it has a unique design. Personally I believe that these "designer pieces" are grossly overpriced in relation to their raw material worth. The proof, in my professional opinion, is that if you wanted to sell this type of jewelry back to the market you would receive only a percentage of the actual silver content value. You would not be paid for the designer's name or the uniqueness of the piece. I would caution you to determine the intrinsic value of the silver jewelry before deciding to purchase an expensive item. You have to ask yourself if the design or the name on the jewelry is worth all that extra money that you are being asked to pay.

To determine the wholesale price of silver jewelry first calculate the intrinsic value. Then add a dollar a gram for any well-made imported piece below 10 grams, 75 cents per gram to any imported piece weighing 10 grams to 25 grams, and 50 cents a gram to any imported piece above 25 grams. I would be very reluctant to pay a higher premium for silver jewelry because it will be impossible to recover unless the price of silver increases very dramatically.

The following three examples will demonstrate how to calculate the wholesale prices of sterling silver jewelry of different weights.

A sterling silver ring weighs 8.50 grams when the price of fine silver is $3.85 per ounce. What should the wholesale price of this ring be? The answer is calculated by first determining the intrinsic value of the pure silver contained in the ring and then adding one dollar per gram for manufacturing and distribution costs.

1. $3.85 (price per ounce of fine silver) divided by 31.1035 grams (number of grams in an ounce) equals .124 cents (price of a gram of fine silver);

2. .124 cents multiplied by 8.50 grams (weight of the ring) equals $1.05 (total intrinsic value of fine silver in the ring);

3. 8.50 grams (weight of ring) multiplied by one dollar (supplemental costs) equals $8.50 (total supplemental costs);

4. $1.52 (total intrinsic value) plus $8.50 (total supplemental costs) equals $10.02 (total wholesale cost of the ring taxes not included).

A pair of sterling silver earrings weighs 13 grams when the price of fine silver is $4.19 per ounce. How much is the wholesale price of these earrings?

1. $4.19 (price per ounce of fine silver) divided by 31.1035 grams (number of grams in an ounce) equals .135 cents (price of a gram of fine silver);
2. .135 cents multiplied by 13 grams (weight of the ring) equals $1.76 (total intrinsic value of fine silver in the ring);
3. 13 grams (weight of ring) multiplied by $.75 (supplemental costs) equals $9.75 (total supplemental costs);
4. $1.76 (total intrinsic value) plus $9.75 (total supplemental costs) equals $11.51 (total wholesale cost of the ring taxes not included).

A sterling silver bracelet weighs 41 grams and the price of pure silver is $4.23 per ounce. What will be the wholesale price of this bracelet?

1. $4.23 (price per ounce of fine silver) divided by 31.1035 grams (number of grams in an ounce) equals .136 cents (price of a gram of fine silver);
2. .136 cents multiplied by 41 grams (weight of bracelet) equals $5.58 (total intrinsic value of fine silver in the bracelet);
3. 41 grams (weight of bracelet) multiplied by $.50 per gram (supplemental costs) equals $20.50 (total supplemental costs);
4. $5.58 (total intrinsic value) plus $20.50 (total supplemental costs) equals $26.08 (total wholesale cost of the bracelet taxes not included).

I have purposely left out one mathematical step in properly calculating the wholesale price of sterling silver jewelry. I did not reduce the total weight of the piece of jewelry by 92.50 percent (the percentage of fine silver contained in sterling silver). The reason for this omission is that the amount of money it represents vis-à-vis the cost of the copper alloy is inconsequential.

CHAPTER 20

Where to Buy Gold Chains

By this time you understand what information is required to determine the intrinsic value of a gold chain as well as its manufacturing and distribution costs. This chapter answers the question, "Where do I go to purchase a desired gold chain?"

Rule 1: Never purchase from a company that refuses to disclose the weight of the gold chain.

If a retail store, catalog showroom, department store, television merchandiser, or discount outlet, etc., does not or will not disclose to you the weight of a chain in grams or pennyweights prior to purchase, *don't buy there.* The reason, as we have previously discussed, is that without knowing the weight of the chain it is impossible to determine the intrinsic value or wholesale price. Without knowing the wholesale price it is impossible to determine how much additional markup (money) you are being asked to pay for the chain by that particular seller.

Rule 2: Determine the country of origin of the gold chain you are interested in purchasing.

There are countries that are more expert in manufacturing machine-made gold chains than other countries. Due to quality, design, and finish, I would currently prefer to purchase chains that are manufactured in Italy, Israel, Germany, the United States, or Canada than from other countries. Most sellers will gladly tell you where the chain was manufactured. If a seller does not know the country of origin, or refuses to divulge the information, *do not purchase there.*

Rule 3: Determine the gold karat of the gold chain you are interested in purchasing.

It is necessary to know the karat of gold used to manufacture the chain so you can determine the intrinsic and wholesale prices. The karat (pure gold percentage) should be stamped somewhere on the chain, normally on or near the clasp. Knowing the country of origin is important in order to be certain that the karat of gold stamped on the chain is trustworthy. If the chain is not stamped or the seller does not clearly state the karatage (fineness) of the chain, *do not purchase from this source.*

Rule 4: Only purchase from a seller who sells his merchandise by weight.

It is customary on the wholesale level in the jewelry trade to purchase gold, machine-made chains by weight. Only on the retail level do the rules change and chains are sold by the piece at very high markups. A knowledgeable consumer will want to purchase from a distributor that sells gold by weight at wholesale prices.

Rule 5: Do not purchase from a seller that wants to charge you retail prices.

As a general rule if you are considering purchasing a gold chain it is reasonable to spend 60 percent above the gold value of that chain. In my opinion, anything above that price is excessive. There are many sellers who would be happy to sell their gold chains at that price. A good place to find such merchants is in the classified Yellow Pages under the heading of *Jewelers— Wholesale.* After finding a few firms that you think might deal in chains, simply call them up and ask the following questions:

1. Do you sell gold chains by weight?
2. How much is your 14-karat price today?
3. How much is an ounce of 24-karat gold?
4. Is this the most current price?

For a full discussion on where to purchase your fine jewelry see Chapter 12. The same principles apply for purchasing fine jewelry as for diamonds; only the merchants are different.

THE ART OF BARGAINING FOR A GOLD CHAIN

You have now assimilated the knowledge and advice covered in the preceding pages and are ready to buy a gold chain. You have also located a jeweler who has your preferred style, karat gold, and length chain and who is willing to sell by weight. This section will cover how to bargain effectively so as to obtain the best possible price.

It is of utmost importance that the jeweler understand that you are knowledgeable. Once the seller realizes that you understand how the wholesale price is determined, the seller will be forced to make you a good deal or risk not making the sale at all. Therefore, it is extremely important that you take control of the conversation early on by asking the right questions.

As a sophisticated consumer, you must have available some pricing information prior to entering a jeweler's establishment. You should know the current price of fine gold. This information is available in the financial section of large newspapers, commodity brokerage firms, coin dealers, gold and silver bullion dealers, precious metal refineries, and larger banks.

You should also calculate the price per gram of the karat gold you are interested in acquiring. For example, if the current price of fine gold is $400 and you are interested in purchasing a 14-karat gold chain, you should calculate the gold price (refer to Appendix A). In this case the price would be $7.50 for a gram of 14-karat gold ($400 divided by 31.1035 equalling $12.86 and then divided by .5833 equalling $7.50 a gram).

Finally, you should calculate the wholesale price by adding 60 percent to the gold price (refer to Chapter 16). In this case the wholesale amount is $12 per gram for 14-karat gold ($7.50 multiplied by 1.6 equals $12).

Now you are ready to start negotiating with the jeweler. After choosing a chain from the merchant's selection, ask for the weight of the chain in grams. This will alert the jeweler that you have some understanding of how to purchase jewelry correctly. Then ask the jeweler to weigh the piece on his gram scale if he has not already done so. This will tell the jeweler that you are not totally trusting. Now ask for the total price of the chain. Write the price down. Now ask the fine gold price the jeweler is using and for the price per gram for 14 karat. Say nothing at this point, but write these amounts down. If the price of gold is not the current price, inquire why the seller is using it. Make certain to point out that you are aware of the current price of gold. This will tell the seller that you have done your homework and you know the rules of the game.

If the price of the 14-karat gold per gram is higher than the calculated wholesale price tell the seller that the price is too expensive. Offer to purchase the chain at 40 percent above the gold or intrinsic price. This will give you 20 percent leeway for negotiations. Remember that you are attempting to purchase jewelry on the wholesale level, where haggling is expected. You're going to have to fight for the most favorable price, so don't be timid or shy. This is a practical game of chess where the opponent is trying to capture as much of your hard-earned money as possible. Your job is to prevent him from taking away any more money than is absolutely necessary.

If you reach an impasse during the negotiations a very effective technique to employ is to say something like, "I really wanted to buy this chain today, but I guess you'd rather hold on to it." With that said show the seller a wad of money and then begin to walk toward the exit door. Most of the time the seller will stop you before you reach the exit and restart the negotiation. Be assured that the jeweler wants to sell the chain. That's why he's there, to sell merchandise and make a profit. Most of the time you can force a better price by knowing the wholesale price and being firm in your approach.

The up side to all this, however, is that it isn't always necessary to bargain in order to get the wholesale price. Just walking into a jeweler carrying this book may be enough of a signal that the merchant will offer the wholesale price.

Most of the principles that are used to purchase gold chains apply equally well to all the other jewelry items. Rings, earrings, pendants, charms, etc., made of gold, platinum, or silver should be purchased by weight. If you apply the principle of intrinsic precious metal value plus reasonable premium charges to your fine jewelry purchases, you will spend fewer dollars to obtain the jewelry you want.

After you have agreed to make a purchase, have the merchant write out a detailed bill of sale and have him sign it. If you are buying a diamond make certain that the size, shape, and quality of the stone are clearly recorded. If the diamond has a corresponding GIA Diamond Grading Report, be certain to include the report number. If you are purchasing fine jewelry include the type of precious metal (gold, platinum, or silver), the degree of purity, and the weight of the piece. I cannot stress enough the importance of having a detailed bill of sale that clearly and definitively describes the item. In the event that a dispute occurs or loss arises this evidentiary document will be the factual basis of any claim.

Easy-to-Use
Precious Metal Price Charts

10-KARAT GOLD 41.67 PERCENT

PRICE	PENNYWEIGHT	GRAM
$150	3.12	2.00
160	3.33	2.14
170	3.54	2.27
180	3.74	2.41
190	3.95	2.54
200	4.16	2.68
210	4.37	2.81
220	4.57	2.94
230	4.78	3.08
240	4.99	3.21
250	5.20	3.34
260	5.41	3.48
270	5.62	3.61
280	5.82	3.74
290	6.03	3.88
300	6.24	4.01
310	6.45	4.15
320	6.66	4.28
330	6.86	4.41
340	7.07	4.55
350	7.28	4.68
360	7.49	4.81
370	7.70	4.95

Price	Pennyweight	Gram
$380	7.90	5.08
390	8.11	5.22
400	8.32	5.35
410	8.53	5.48
420	8.74	5.62
430	8.94	5.75
440	9.15	5.88
450	9.36	6.02
460	9.57	6.15
470	9.78	6.27
480	9.98	6.42
490	10.19	6.55
500	10.40	6.69
510	10.61	6.82
520	10.82	6.95
530	11.02	7.09
540	11.23	7.22
550	11.44	7.35
560	11.65	7.49
570	11.86	7.62
580	12.96	7.76
590	12.27	7.89
600	12.48	8.02
610	12.69	8.16
620	12.90	8.29
630	13.10	8.43
640	13.31	8.56
650	13.52	8.69
660	13.73	8.83
670	13.94	8.96
680	14.14	9.09
690	14.35	9.23
700	14.56	9.36

PRICE	PENNYWEIGHT	GRAM
$710	14.77	9.50
720	14.98	9.63
730	15.18	9.76
740	15.39	9.90
750	15.60	10.03
760	15.81	10.16
770	16.02	10.30
780	16.22	10.43
790	16.43	10.57
800	16.64	10.70

Formulas used:

Pennyweight Price = Gold Price ÷ 20 × .416

Gram Price = Gold Price ÷ 31.1035 × .416

There are 20 pennyweights (dwt) to ounce; 31.1035 grams to ounce.

14-KARAT GOLD 58.33 PERCENT

PRICE	PENNYWEIGHT	GRAM
$150	4.37	2.81
160	4.66	3.00
170	4.96	3.19
180	5.25	3.37
190	5.54	3.56
200	5.83	3.75
210	6.12	3.93
220	6.41	4.12
230	6.70	4.31
240	7.00	4.50
250	7.29	4.69
260	7.58	4.87
270	7.87	5.06
280	8.16	5.25
290	8.45	5.44
300	8.75	5.62
310	9.04	5.81
320	9.33	6.00
330	9.62	6.19
340	9.91	6.37
350	10.20	6.56
360	10.49	6.75
370	10.79	6.93
380	11.08	7.12
390	11.37	7.31
400	11.66	7.50
410	11.95	7.68
420	12.24	7.87
430	12.53	8.06
440	12.82	8.25
450	13.12	8.43

Price	Pennyweight	Gram
$460	13.41	8.62
470	13.70	8.81
480	13.99	9.00
490	14.28	9.18
500	14.58	9.37
510	14.87	9.56
520	15.16	9.75
530	15.45	9.93
540	15.74	10.12
550	16.03	10.31
560	16.32	10.50
570	16.62	10.68
580	16.91	10.87
590	17.20	11.06
600	17.49	11.25
610	17.78	11.43
620	18.07	11.62
630	18.36	11.81
640	18.66	12.00
650	18.95	12.18
660	19.24	12.37
670	19.53	12.56
680	19.82	12.75
690	20.11	12.93
700	20.40	13.12
710	20.70	13.31
720	20.99	13.50
730	21.28	13.68
740	21.57	13.87
750	21.86	14.06
760	22.15	14.25
770	22.45	14.43
780	22.74	14.62

PRICE	PENNYWEIGHT	GRAM
$790	23.03	14.81
800	23.32	15.00

Formulas used:

Pennyweight Price = Gold Price ÷ 20 × .583

Gram Price = Gold Price ÷ 31.1035 × .583

There are 20 dwt to ounce; 31.1035 grams to ounce.

18-KARAT GOLD 75.00 PERCENT

PRICE	PENNYWEIGHT	GRAM
$150	5.63	3.62
160	6.00	3.86
170	6.38	4.10
180	6.75	4.34
190	7.13	4.58
200	7.50	4.82
210	7.88	5.06
220	8.25	5.30
230	8.63	5.55
240	9.00	5.79
250	9.38	6.03
260	9.75	6.27
270	10.13	6.51
280	10.50	6.75
290	10.88	6.99
300	11.25	7.23
310	11.63	7.48
320	12.00	7.72
330	12.38	7.96
340	12.75	8.20
350	13.13	8.44
360	13.50	8.68
370	13.88	8.92
380	14.25	9.16
390	14.63	9.40
400	15.00	9.64
410	15.38	9.89
420	15.75	10.13
430	16.13	10.37
440	16.50	10.61
450	16.88	10.85

Price	Pennyweight	Gram
$460	17.25	11.09
470	17.63	11.33
480	18.00	11.57
490	18.38	11.82
500	18.75	12.06
510	19.13	12.30
520	19.50	12.54
530	19.88	12.78
540	20.25	13.02
550	20.63	13.26
560	21.00	13.50
570	21.38	13.74
580	21.75	13.99
590	22.13	14.23
600	22.50	14.47
610	22.88	14.71
620	23.25	14.95
630	23.63	15.19
640	24.00	15.43
650	24.38	15.67
660	24.75	15.91
670	25.13	16.16
680	25.50	16.40
690	25.88	16.64
700	26.25	16.88
710	26.63	17.12
720	27.00	17.36
730	27.38	17.60
740	27.75	17.84
750	28.13	18.08
760	28.50	18.33
770	28.88	18.56
780	29.25	18.81

PRICE	PENNYWEIGHT	GRAM
$790	29.63	19.05
800	30.00	19.29

Formulas used:

Pennyweight Price = Gold Price ÷ 20 × .750

Gram Price = Gold Price ÷ 31.1035 × .750

There are 20 dwt to ounce; 31.1035 grams to ounce.

24-KARAT GOLD

PRICE	PENNYWEIGHT	GRAM
$150	7.50	4.82
160	8.00	5.14
170	8.50	5.47
180	9.00	5.79
190	9.50	6.11
200	10.00	6.43
210	10.50	6.75
220	11.00	7.07
230	11.50	7.39
240	12.00	7.72
250	12.50	8.04
260	13.00	8.36
270	13.50	8.68
280	14.00	9.00
290	14.50	9.32
300	15.00	9.64
310	15.50	9.97
320	16.00	10.29
330	16.50	10.61
340	17.00	10.93
350	17.50	11.25
360	18.00	11.57
370	18.50	11.90
380	19.00	12.22
390	19.50	12.54
400	20.00	12.86
410	20.50	13.18
420	21.00	13.50
430	21.50	13.82
440	22.00	14.15
450	22.50	14.47

Price	Pennyweight	Gram
$460	23.00	14.79
470	23.50	15.11
480	24.00	15.43
490	24.50	15.75
500	25.00	16.08
510	25.50	16.40
520	26.00	16.72
530	26.50	17.04
540	27.00	17.36
550	27.50	17.68
560	28.00	18.00
570	28.50	18.32
580	29.00	18.65
590	29.50	18.97
600	30.00	19.29
610	30.50	19.61
620	31.00	19.93
630	31.50	20.25
640	32.00	20.58
650	32.50	20.90
660	33.00	21.22
670	33.50	21.54
680	34.00	21.86
690	34.50	22.18
700	35.00	22.50
710	35.50	22.83
720	36.00	23.15
730	36.50	23.47
740	37.00	23.79
750	37.50	24.11
760	38.00	24.43
770	38.50	24.76
780	39.00	25.08

Price	Pennyweight	Gram
$790	39.50	25.40
800	40.00	25.72

Formulas used:

Pennyweight Price = Gold Price ÷ 20

Gram Price = Gold Price ÷ 31.1035

There are 20 dwt to ounce; 31.1035 grams to ounce.

PLATINUM

Price	Pennyweight	Gram
$150	7.50	4.82
160	8.00	5.14
170	8.50	5.47
180	9.00	5.79
190	9.50	6.11
200	10.00	6.43
210	10.50	6.75
220	11.00	7.07
230	11.50	7.39
240	12.00	7.72
250	12.50	8.04
260	13.00	8.36
270	13.50	8.68
280	14.00	9.00
290	14.50	9.32
300	15.00	9.64
310	15.50	9.97
320	16.00	10.29
330	16.50	10.61
340	17.00	10.93
350	17.50	11.25
360	18.00	11.57
370	18.50	11.90
380	19.00	12.22
390	19.50	12.54
400	20.00	12.86
410	20.50	13.18
420	21.00	13.50
430	21.50	13.82
440	22.00	14.15
450	22.50	14.47

Price	Pennyweight	Gram
$460	23.00	14.79
470	23.50	15.11
480	24.00	15.43
490	24.50	15.75
500	25.00	16.08
510	25.50	16.40
520	26.00	16.72
530	26.50	17.04
540	27.00	17.36
550	27.50	17.68
560	28.00	18.00
570	28.50	18.32
580	29.00	18.65
590	29.50	18.97
600	30.00	19.29
610	30.50	19.61
620	31.00	19.93
630	31.50	20.25
640	32.00	20.58
650	32.50	20.90
660	33.00	21.22
670	33.50	21.54
680	34.00	21.86
690	34.50	22.18
700	35.00	22.50
710	35.50	22.83
720	36.00	23.15
730	36.50	23.47
740	37.00	23.79
750	37.50	24.11
760	38.00	24.43
770	38.50	24.76
780	39.00	25.08

Price	Pennyweight	Gram
$790	39.50	25.40
800	40.00	25.72

Formulas used:

Pennyweight Price = Platinum Price ÷ 20

Gram Price = Platinum Price ÷ 31.1035

There are 20 dwt to ounce; 31.1035 grams to ounce.

STERLING SILVER

Price	Pennyweight	Gram
$3.00	.14	.09
3.10	.14	.09
3.20	.15	.10
3.30	.15	.10
3.40	.16	.10
3.50	.16	.11
3.60	.17	.11
3.70	.17	.11
3.80	.18	.11
3.90	.18	.12
4.00	.19	.12
4.10	.19	.12
4.20	.19	.12
4.30	.20	.12
4.40	.20	.13
4.50	.21	.13
4.60	.21	.13
4.70	.22	.14
4.80	.22	.14
4.90	.23	.14
5.00	.23	.15
5.10	.23	.15
5.20	.24	.15
5.30	.24	.16
5.40	.25	.16
5.50	.25	.16
5.60	.26	.17
5.70	.26	.17
5.80	.27	.17
5.90	.27	.17
6.00	.28	.18

PRICE	PENNYWEIGHT	GRAM
$6.10	.28	.18
6.20	.29	.18
6.30	.29	.19
6.40	.30	.19
6.50	.30	.19
6.60	.31	.20
6.70	.31	.20
6.80	.31	.20
6.90	.32	.20
7.00	.32	.21
7.10	.33	.21
7.20	.33	.21
7.30	.34	.22
7.40	.34	.22
7.50	.35	.22
7.60	.35	.23
7.70	.35	.23
7.80	.36	.23
7.90	.36	.23
8.00	.37	.24
8.10	.37	.24
8.20	.38	.24
8.30	.38	.25
8.40	.39	.25
8.50	.39	.25
8.60	.40	.25
8.70	.40	.26
8.80	.41	.26
8.90	.41	.26
9.00	.42	.27
9.10	.42	.27
9.20	.42	.27
9.30	.43	.28

Price	Pennyweight	Gram
$9.40	.43	.28
9.50	.44	.28
9.60	.44	.28
9.70	.45	.29
9.80	.45	.29
9.90	.46	.29
10.00	.46	.30

Formulas used:

Pennyweight Price = Silver Price ÷ 20

Gram Price = Silver Price ÷ 31.1035

The Mathematics of Diamonds and Fine Jewelry

1. You are interested in purchasing a well-proportioned, round, brilliant-cut diamond weighing 1.37 carats, having a color grade of G and a clarity grade of VS2. The New York wholesale asking price of this stone is $6,100 (Rapaport Diamond Report 2/7/97). How much is the total cost of this diamond?

1.37 carats × $6,100 = $8,357

2. You are thinking of purchasing a diamond tennis bracelet having a total diamond weight of 10 carats. The bracelet has fifty stones that are all uniform in size and weight. How much does each diamond weigh?

There are 100 points to a carat. 10.00 carats equals 1,000 points. 1,000 points divided by 50 stones equals .20 points or 1/5 of a carat each.

3. A jeweler is trying to sell a 1.90 carat marquise-shape diamond for $11,500. The diamond is well proportioned, having the color grade of I and the clarity grade SI1. Is this a good deal (use Rapaport Diamond Report 2/7/97)?

According to Rapaport the New York asking price for the marquise diamond is $4,800 per carat. The price is determined by multiplying the weight of the diamond by its per-carat price. 1.90 ct. × $4,800 = $9,120. The price the jeweler is asking is $2,300 higher than Rapaport. You should be able to purchase this diamond 20 percent above the Rapaport price, which is $10,944 (9,120 × 1.20 = $10,944), so this is not a good deal.

4. You are thinking of buying a well-made 3.00-carat emerald-cut diamond. The stone has a color grade of J, a clarity grade of I1, and has been laser treated. The discount for a lasered diamond is 20 percent. How much does this gem cost (use Rapaport Diamond Report 2/7/97)?

According to Rapaport the New York asking price for a well-made emerald-shape diamond is $3,300 per carat. Since this stone must be discounted 20 percent because of the laser treatment the per-carat price is reduced to $2,640 (3,300 × .80 = $2,640). The total price of the diamond is $7,920 (3.00 cts. × $2,640 = $7,940).

5. A 14-karat neckchain is 16 inches long and weighs 19 grams. The current price for pure (24-karat) gold is $343 per ounce. Using my recommendations what is the most you should pay for this chain?

A. Determine the price of one gram of pure or 24-karat gold. $343 divided by 31.1035 grams (grams in an ounce) = $11.03 per gram.

B. Determine the price of one gram of 14-karat gold. Fourteen-karat gold is 58.35 percent pure gold. $11.03 × .5835 = $6.43 (price of one gram of 14 karat when fine gold is $343 per ounce).

C. To determine the gold value or intrinsic value of this chain you multiply the weight of the chain by the price of the 14-karat gold. The gold or intrinsic value of this chain is $122.17 (19 grams × $6.43 = $122.17).

D. The premium that needs to be added to the intrinsic value of this chain will cover the costs of manufacture, distribution, overheads, profits, etc. I have recommended allowing an additional 60 percent for these expenses. Therefore, the price of this machine-made chain should be $195.47 ($122.17 × 1.60 = $195.47).

6. You would like to purchase an 18-karat gold ring that weighs 11 grams. The current price of gold is $452. Using my guidelines what is the most you should pay for this ring?

A. Determine the price of one gram of pure or 24-karat gold. $452 divided by 31.1035 grams (grams in an ounce) = $14.53 per gram.

B. Determine the price of one gram of 18-karat gold. Eighteen-karat gold is 75 percent pure gold. $14.53 × .75 = $10.90 (price of one gram of 18 karat when fine gold is $452 per ounce).

C. To determine the gold or intrinsic value of this ring you multiply the weight of the ring by the price of the 18-karat gold. The gold or intrinsic value of this ring is $119.90 (11 grams × $10.90) = $119.90).

D. The premium that needs to be added to the intrinsic value of this ring will cover the costs of manufacture, distribution, overheads, profits, etc. I have recommended allowing an additional 125 percent for these expenses. Therefore, the price of this casted ring should be $269.78 ($119.90 × 2.25 = $269.78).

7. You want to purchase a pair of 14-karat earrings that weighs 5 grams. The current price of gold is $340. Using my guidelines what is the most you should pay for these earrings?

A. Determine the price of one gram of pure or 24-karat gold. $340 divided by 31.1035 grams (grams in an ounce) = $10.93 per gram.

B. Determine the price of one gram of 14-karat gold. Fourteen-karat gold is 58.35 percent pure gold. $10.93 × .5835 = $6.38 (price of one gram of 14 karat when fine gold is $340 per ounce).

C. To determine the gold or intrinsic value of these earrings you multiply the weight of the earrings by the price of the 14-karat gold. The gold or intrinsic value of these earrings is $31.90 (5 grams × $6.38 = $31.90).

D. The premium that needs to be added to the intrinsic value of this ring will cover the costs of manufacture, distribution, overheads, profits, etc. I have recommended allowing an additional 125 percent for these expenses. Therefore, the price of these earrings should be $71.78 ($31.90 × 2.25 = $71.78).

8. You want to purchase a 10-karat bracelet that weighs 15 grams. The current price of pure gold is $381. Using my guidelines what is the most you should pay for this bracelet?

A. Determine the price of one gram of pure or 24-karat gold. $381 divided by 31.1035 grams (grams in an ounce) = $12.24 per gram.

B. Determine the price of one gram of 10-karat gold. Ten-karat gold is 41.67 percent pure gold. $12.24 ×

.4167 = $5.10 (price of one gram of 10 karat when fine gold is $381 per ounce).

C. To determine the gold or intrinsic value of this bracelet you multiply the weight of the bracelet by the price of the 10-karat gold. The gold or intrinsic value of this bracelet is $76.50 (15 grams × $5.10 = $76.50).

D. The premium that needs to be added to the intrinsic value of this ring will cover the costs of manufacture, distribution, overheads, profits, etc. I have recommended allowing an additional 100 percent for these expenses. Therefore, the price of this bracelet should be $153.00 (76.50 × 2.00 = $153.00).

9. You want to buy a ring that weighs 8 grams and is hallmarked "90%Plat10%Irid." The current price of pure platinum is $397 per ounce. Using my guidelines what is the most you should pay for this ring?

A. Determine the price of one gram of pure platinum. $397 divided by 31.1035 grams (grams in an ounce) = $12.76 per gram.

B. To determine the platinum or intrinsic value of this ring you multiply the weight of the ring by the price of the platinum per gram. The intrinsic value of this ring is $102.11 (8 grams × $12.76 = $102.11).

C. The premium that needs to be added to the intrinsic value of this platinum ring will cover the costs of manufacture, distribution, overheads, profits, etc. I have recommended allowing 150 percent premium for these expenses. Therefore, the price of this ring should be $255.27 ($102.11 × 2.50 = $255.27).

10. You want to purchase an imported sterling silver bracelet that weighs 32 grams. The current price of pure silver is $3.21 per ounce. Using my guidelines what is the most you should pay for this bracelet?

A. Determine the price of one gram of pure silver. $3.21 divided by 31.1035 grams (grams in an ounce) = $.103 per gram.

B. To determine the silver or intrinsic value of this bracelet you multiply the weight of the bracelet by the price of the silver per gram. The intrinsic value of this bracelet is $3.30 (32 grams × $.103 = $3.30).

C. The premium that needs to be added to the intrinsic value of this imported bracelet will cover the costs of manufacture, distribution, overheads, profits, etc. I have recommended allowing an additional $.50 per gram for these expenses. Therefore, the price of this bracelet should be $19.30 (32 grams × $.50 = $16.00, $16.00 + $3.30 = $19.30).

APPENDIX C

Important Addresses with Telephone and Fax Numbers

Frank J. Adler
P.O. Box 611802
Miami, Florida 33261-1802
Telephone: (305) 891-0000
Fax: (305) 864-3075
E-Mail: Farower@aol.com

The American Gem Society
8881 W. Sahara Avenue
Las Vegas, Nevada 89117-5865
Telephone: (702) 255-6500
Fax: (702) 255-7420

GIA Gem Trade Laboratory
580 Fifth Avenue
New York, New York 10036-4794
Telephone: (212) 221-5858
Fax: (212) 575-3095

GIA Gem Trade Laboratory
5355 Armada Drive
Carlsbad, California 92008-4699
Telephone: (760) 603-4500
Fax: (760) 603-1814

196

The International Society of Appraisers
16040 Christensen Road, Suite 320
Seattle, Washington 98188-2929
Telephone: (206) 241-0359
Fax: (206) 241-0436

National Association of Jewelry Appraisers
P.O. Box 6558
Annapolis, Maryland 21401-0558
Telephone: (301) 261-8270

Rapaport Diamond Report
15 W. 47th Street
New York, New York 10036-3305
Telephone: (212) 354-0575
Fax: (212) 840-0243

Abbreviations of Jewelry Terminology

AGS: American Gem Society

Ct: Carat (pertaining to diamonds)

Cts: Carats (pertaining to diamonds)

Dwt: Pennyweight (in the troy system of weights)

F: Flawless (GIA clarity grading system for diamonds)

GG: Graduate gemologist (highest degree awarded by GIA)

GIA: Gemological Institute of America

I: Imperfect (GIA clarity grading system for diamonds)

IF: Internally Flawless (GIA clarity grading system for diamonds)

K: Karat (the fineness of gold)

SI: Slightly Imperfect (GIA clarity grading system for diamonds)

VS: Very Slightly Imperfect (GIA clarity grading system for diamonds)

VVS: Very, Very Slightly Imperfect (GIA clarity grading system for diamonds)

Glossary

AGS Abbreviation for "American Gem Society."

Alloy A compound metal resulting from melting together two or more metals. Fourteen-karat gold, for example, is an alloy composed of 58.34 percent fine gold and 41.66 percent other metals such as silver, copper, zinc, or nickel.

Appraiser One who estimates the size, quality, and value in terms of currency of an object such as a diamond or a piece of fine jewelry.

Automatic weaving equipment Machinery used to manufacture chains made of precious metal that are worn around the neck, ankle, or arm.

Avoirdupois weight A system of weight used in the United States in which one pound avoirdupois equals 16 ounces. This system of weight is not used for precious metals or diamonds.

Baguette A square-cornered, rectangular-shaped diamond with rows of steplike facets.

Blemish Any imperfection, such as a scratch or minor crack, on the surface of a polished diamond.

Body color The natural color of a diamond.

Bourse An exchange or meeting place where diamond merchants conduct business.

Bracelet An item of jewelry normally worn around the wrist.

Brilliancy The total amount of light reflected from the interior and exterior surfaces of a diamond.

Brilliant-cut (round) The most common style of cutting a diamond that allows the optimum brilliancy to be displayed. The standard round brilliant-cut consists of 58 facets.

Burnout furnace   A piece of equipment used in the lost-wax casting process to evaporate the wax pattern placed in the investment.

Burnout procedure   A step in the lost-wax casting process that allows the wax pattern to be eliminated in the investment.

Carat   A unit of weight for diamonds that equals one-fifth of a gram or 200 milligrams. A five-carat diamond weighs one gram.

Caster   A caster reproduces a metal form from a wax pattern by using the lost-wax process. A caster normally cuts rubber molds, makes wax patterns, and produces metallic replicas of the wax patterns.

Casting   An unfinished piece of jewelry formed by pouring molten metal into a form.

Certified Appraisers of Personal Property   A title bestowed by The International Society of Appraisers recognizing a professional competence in gemology.

Certified Gemologist Appraiser   A title granted by the American Gem Society signifying professional expertise in the area of gemology.

Charm   A trinket that is worn on a chain, bracelet, etc.

Clarity Grade   The relative position of cleanliness of a diamond based on a grading scale developed by the GIA. The scale ranges from flawless to imperfect.

Cobalt   A non-precious metal that is sometimes used to alloy platinum.

Color Grade   The relative position of body color of a diamond based on a grading scale developed by the GIA. The scale ranges from D (colorless) to Z (yellow).

Colorless   The rarest and most expensive diamonds are the absolutely colorless ones.

Crown   The portion of a diamond above the girdle, the top one-third of the stone.

Crown angle　The angle at which the upper portion of the diamond is cut.

Culet　The lowest point of the diamond that is sometimes polished parallel to the table.

Cut　A term used to describe the quality of the manufacturing of a diamond.

De Beers Consolidated Mines, Ltd.　The company, known as "The Syndicate," that purchases and controls the distribution of most the world's rough (uncut) diamonds.

Depth percentage　The measurement from the top (table) to the bottom (culet) divided by the average diameter at the girdle. This is an important factor in determining how well a diamond has been manufactured.

Designer　An artist who develops a preliminary plan or sketch for a new model.

Diamond　A mineral composed of carbon that is crystallized by intense heat and pressure.

Diamond dealer　A merchant who sells diamonds on the wholesale level to jewelry manufacturers, retailers, or other dealers.

Diamond Grading Report (GIA)　A report issued by the GIA that accurately describes the size, quality, and shape of a diamond.

Diamond setting　Securely and permanently placing a diamond into a piece of jewelry.

Dies　Specific metal forms used in the stamping process to reproduce certain needed shapes.

Dwt.　An abbreviation for pennyweight, a unit of weight in the troy system.

Earrings　Jewelry that is normally worn on the ears.

Emerald cut　A rectangular, step-cut stone with sharp, squared-off corners.

Emerald-cut diamond　A fancy-shape diamond that is cut in a rectangular shape having sharp corners and rows (steps) of elongated facets on the crown and pavilion that are parallel to the girdle.

Engagement ring   A ring given as a symbol of betrothal, normally a diamond solitaire.

Facet   A flat polished surface on a diamond.

Fancy cut   Any shape of a polished diamond other than a round stone.

Findings   Standard parts such as clasps or earring posts that are used in the manufacturing of jewelry.

Findings dealer   A merchant who sells findings on the wholesale level to jewelry manufacturers, retailers, or other dealers.

Fine gold   Gold that is totally pure or 24-karat gold. Gold that does not contain any other metal.

Fineness   The purity of the gold. For example, 18-karat gold is 75 percent pure gold or has the fineness of 75 percent.

Finish   Refers to the symmetry (how the facets of the crown and pavilion are aligned) and the final polish of a cut diamond.

Fire (scintillation)   The separation of white light into the various colors of the spectrum caused by the prism effect of diamonds on the light passing through the stones. It also refers to the radiance of the sparkle of a diamond.

Fish-eye   A diamond whose pavilion is extremely shallow, producing a stone with an obvious lack of brilliance.

Flaw   Any internal or external imperfection on a polished diamond.

Flawless (F)   A diamond that possesses no internal or external imperfections. The highest grade awarded to a diamond for clarity based on the GIA clarity grading system.

Fracture filling   A method whereby a crack in a diamond is filled with liquid glass to enhance its clarity.

Gem   A stone of beauty that is cut and polished and used in jewelry.

Gemologist   One who has studied and become an expert in gemstones.

Gemologist-appraiser   An expert in gems who issues appraisals as to quality, size, authenticity, and possible monetary value.

Girdle   The dividing line between the top (crown) and bottom (pavilion) portion of a diamond which forms the outer edge or perimeter.

Gold   A yellow-colored metallic element that is impervious to corrosion and oxidation.

Gold value   The monetary value of the total fine gold contained in a piece of jewelry.

Graduate Gemologist (GG)   A degree awarded by the Gemological Institute of America for successful completion of their course of study in gemology.

Hallmark   An official mark stamped on gold, silver, and platinum articles indicating their standards of purity, origin, and maker.

Heart-shape diamond   A fancy-shape diamond cut in the form of a heart.

Imperfect (I)   The lowest grade a diamond can be awarded in the clarity grading system devised by the GIA. Describes a diamond with serious and perhaps visible inclusions.

Imperfection   Any internal or external flaw on a cut and polished diamond.

Inclusion   A term that refers to any visible foreign object in a diamond.

Insurance   An offsetting guarantee against risk of loss, harm, or death.

Insurance appraisal   A document proving the size, quality, or monetary worth of an object, such as a diamond, written for insurance purposes.

Internally Flawless (IF)   The second highest grade a diamond can be awarded in the clarity grading system devised by the GIA. A diamond without any internal flaws but with minor surface blemishes that may be removed.

Internet   A worldwide communication system comprised of thousands of computers linked together.

Intrinsic value The monetary value of the total precious metal (gold, platinum, or silver) contained in a piece of fine jewelry.

Investment A plaster of Paris–type material used in the lost-wax casting process.

Iridium A precious metal, part of the platinum metal group, that is sometimes used to alloy platinum.

Jeweler A craftsperson that makes or repairs fine jewelry.

Jewelry manufacturer A person or company that fabricates jewelry or produces some standard parts used in the jewelry industry (findings).

Karat Indicates the amount of pure gold present in a piece of gold jewelry.

Karat gold A mixture of pure gold melted together with other metals to form a usable alloy such as 10-, 14-, or 18-karat gold.

Laser drilling A process used to enhance the clarity of a diamond by drilling a hole with a laser beam and bleaching a dark crystal white.

Lost-wax casting process The modern method for forming fine jewelry by burning out (vaporizing) mass-produced wax patterns and forcing molten metal into duplicated cavities in a plaster of Paris–type material.

Loupe A small, hand-held, ten-power magnifying glass.

Make Refers to the quality of the proportions and finish of a polished diamond.

Marquise-cut diamond A fancy-cut diamond with two points and a boat-shaped girdle.

Master The original metal model of a jewelry design made by the model maker and used to make all subsequent rubber molds.

Metal stamping process A procedure during which stamping machines (presses) and steel dies are used to create various shaped forms out of metal.

Model maker A jewelry craftsperson who makes an original jewelry design out of carving wax or metal. This design is normally copied from a rendering and is called the master.

Mold maker   A craftsperson who utilizes the master to make rubber molds that are used in the lost-wax casting process.

Net profit   In business, the amount of money that remains after all expenses are paid.

Out-of-round diamond   Refers to a diamond where the circumference or girdle deviates from being perfectly round.

Oval-cut diamond   A fancy-shape, brilliant-cut diamond with an elliptical outline.

Overhead   All the general costs that are incurred in order to own and operate a business except for the actual cost of purchasing inventory.

Palladium   A precious metal, part of the platinum metal group, that is sometimes used to alloy platinum.

Pavilion   The part of a diamond below the girdle.

Pear-shape diamond   A fancy-shape, brilliant-cut diamond with a pear-shaped girdle silhouette.

Pendants   A category of jewelry that is a hanging ornament and normally worn on a chain around the neck.

Pennyweight   A unit of weight equivalent to 1/20 of a troy ounce.

Platinum   A heavy, light gray precious metal that is normally alloyed with iridium or cobalt.

Point   A unit of diamond weight equivalent to 1/100 of a carat.

Polish (jewelry)   The process whereby a piece of jewelry is brought to a radiant luster. It is normally the last process to be employed when manufacturing or finishing a piece of jewelry.

Polisher   A craftsman who finishes the jewelry by brightening the metal and removing minor faults and blemishes.

Precious metal casters   A modern-day caster reproduces a metal form from a wax pattern by using the lost-wax process.

Proportions   In a diamond, proportions refer to the quality and exactness with which a stone is cut or polished. Proportions can encompass depth and table percentage, roundness, and crown angles.

Rapaport Diamond Report   A list that monitors the New York wholesale asking price for diamonds.

Renderings   In jewelry, a designer's detailed sketches of a new jewelry design.

Retail   The sale of merchandise to the ultimate consumer.

Retail replacement cost   For insurance purposes, the cost of replacing a commodity, such as a diamond, if purchased through a retailer at retail prices.

Rubber mold   In the lost-wax casting process, the metal master is used to manufacture a rubber mold which allows exact replica wax patterns of the master to be reproduced over and over again for mass production.

Ruthenium   A precious metal, part of the platinum metal group, that is sometimes used to alloy platinum.

Scintillation (fire)   The separation of white light into the various colors of the spectrum caused by the prism effect of diamonds on the light passing through the stones. It also refers to the radiance of the sparkle of a diamond.

Setter   A craftsperson who specializes in safely and securely placing a diamond permanently in a piece of fine jewelry.

Shallow diamond   A stone whose pavilion is cut too shallow will lose brilliancy and will have a glassy appearance.

Silver   A white precious metal that is used to make fine jewelry.

Slightly Imperfect (SI)   The fifth highest grade a diamond can be awarded in the clarity grading system devised by the GIA.

Spread diamond   A stone that has been cut with a large table and a thin crown to appear larger in weight than it really is.

Stamping   The process of forming metal for jewelry by using a powerful machine called a stamping press and steel dies.

Sterling silver   A precious metal alloy consisting of $92^1/_2$ percent pure silver and $7^1/_2$ percent pure copper.

Symmetry   In a diamond, whether or not the facets are properly aligned one to another.

Table   The top facet on the crown of a diamond that is large and flat.

Table percentage   In a round, brilliant-cut diamond the measurement that determines the relationship of the table to the width of the stone. A large table indicates a spread diamond, and a small table indicates a thick stone that appears smaller than its actual weight. Both cuts cause a loss of brilliance or fire.

Troy weight   A system of weights used for gold and silver in the United States and Great Britain in which 1 pound equals 12 ounces and 1 ounce equals 20 pennyweights.

Very Slightly Imperfect (VS)   The fourth highest grade a diamond can be awarded in the clarity grading system devised by the GIA.

Very, Very Slightly Imperfect (VVS)   The third highest grade a diamond can be awarded in the clarity grading system devised by the GIA.

Wholesale   The prices that retailers pay for merchandise or prices significantly discounted below retail prices.

Index

ABOUT THE AUTHOR

FRANK J. ADLER has been involved in various phases of the jewelry business for three decades. His career has included work as a diamond dealer, a colored stone dealer, a manufacturer of fine gold and diamond jewelry, an estate buyer, a gold and silver bullion dealer, and a refiner of precious metals for the jewelry trade. He has purchased diamonds in Europe and the Middle East, pearls and jade in Hong Kong, colored stones in Germany and the Far East, and fine gold jewelry in France and England.

Mr. Adler has a Bachelor of Arts degree from Pennsylvania State University and has a Diamond Grading and Evaluation degree from the Gemological Institute of America.